*Law*Basics

FAMILY LAW

Other titles in the Series

Agency
Commercial Law
Constitutional Law
Contract
Evidence
Scottish Legal System
Succession
Trusts

AUSTRALIA
LBC Information Services
Sydney

CANADA AND THE USA
Carswell
Toronto

NEW ZEALAND
Brooker's
Auckland

*Law*Basics

FAMILY LAW

By

Elaine E. Sutherland, LL.B., LL.M.

Senior Lecturer in Private Law,
University of Glasgow and Professor of Law,
Northwestern School of Law of Lewis and
Clark College, Portland, Oregon

EDINBURGH
W. GREEN/Sweet & Maxwell
1999

First published 1999
Reprinted 2003

Published in 1999 by W. Green & Son Limited of
21 Alva Street,
Edinburgh EH2 4PS

Typeset by Servis Filmsetting Ltd, Manchester, England

Printed in Great Britain by
Creative Print and Design (Wales), Ebbw Vale

No natural forests were destroyed to make this product; only farmed timber
was used ad replanted

A CIP catalogue record of this book is available from the British Library

ISBN 0 414 01232 1

CONTENTS

TABLE OF CASES

succession rights in the father's estate (Human Fertilisation and Embryology Act 1990, s. 28(6)(b)).

Ante-natal injury
An important application of the *nasciturus* principle is in the context of ante-natal injury. Where a child is born with disabilities as a result of something that happened before birth, the child can recover damages for the injuries from the person responsible for them. So, for example, where the hospital staff are negligent in delivering a baby and their negligence results in injury, the child will be able to recover damages for his or her injuries. When it examined the question in 1973, the Scottish Law Commission was so confident that this was already the position in Scots law that it believed there was no need to legislate on the matter (*Report on Liability for Antenatal Injury* (1973)). This contrasts with the position in England and Wales where recovery for antenatal injury is governed by statute (Congenital Disabilities (Civil Liability) Act 1976).

Whether the child's mother could be liable for ante-natal injury remains unlitigated, as yet, in Scotland. Clearly, a pregnant woman is in a unique position in relation to the foetus she is carrying and, applying general delictual principles, where she knows or ought to know that something she is doing is likely to cause injury to the foetus and the resulting child, she will be liable. The Scottish Law Commission was in no doubt that such recovery was competent (*Report on Liability for Antenatal Injury* (1973)). The only real case against maternal liability for ante-natal injury lies in public policy. It has been variously argued that to accept such liability would create friction between the child and the mother; that no real benefit would accrue to the child, since any damages would come from the family coffers; that liability would place unreasonable restrictions on the freedom of action of pregnant women; and that it would give foetal rights priority over the rights of women. It has been suggested that some women might seek abortions in order to avoid liability, although there is no evidence to support such a notion. While maternal liability for ante-natal injury has been accepted in other jurisdictions (*Grodin v. Grodin* (1981) (USA); *Lynch v. Lynch* (1992) (NSW, Australia)), acceptance is far from universal (*Stallman v. Youngquist* (1985) (USA)).

Where a child is born alive and thus acquires legal personality, this can have implications for the parents' right to recover damages for the child's subsequent death. The Damages (Scotland) Act 1976, s. 1(1) gives certain relatives of a person who dies as a result of his or her injuries the right to recover from the person responsible for the injuries. In *Hamilton v. Fife Health Board* (1992 and 1993), the parents of a child who died at three days old as a result of negligent delivery procedures were successful in recovering damages. The view was taken in the Outer House that, since there was no possible benefit to the deceased child, the *nasciturus* principle could not apply. On appeal, the decision was reversed by the Inner House, where the court proceeded on the basis that the child's right to raise an action had accrued when the child was born alive and that the parents, as relatives, had a right to recover under the 1976 Act. In taking the view that it was not necessary to apply the *nasciturus* principle in order to achieve this result, the court was following an earlier Outer House decision (*Mc Williams v. Lord Advocate* (1992)) where recovery was allowed in similar circumstances without resort to the *nasciturus* principle.

Recognition and regulation of the ante-natal environment
Child protection legislation recognises the ante-natal situation in looking at prior parental conduct when considering whether a child born today may be at risk. Any prior behaviour may be relevant including parental treatment of a previous child and the mother's conduct while she was pregnant. It is competent for the local authority to seek a child protection order in respect of a child where the child has never lived with the parents, but where their past conduct suggests that the child is likely to suffer significant harm and that the order is necessary to protect the child. The case will then be referred to the children's reporter who may arrange a children's hearing (see chapters 6 and 7).

Recognition of the ante-natal environment raises the question of *regulating* that environment. Clearly, the birth of healthy children is a desirable goal and thus, for example, the State accepts a responsibility to serve that goal by providing ante-natal education and health care. Whether the legal system should go further by, for example, incarcerating pregnant women who persist in drug abuse, has been hotly debated in other jurisdictions. To date, the Scottish courts have not had the opportunity to address the issue of whether a competent, conscious woman should be compelled to undergo a Caesarean delivery against her wishes. Since the general principle is that the consent of a competent patient is a prerequisite to medical treatment, it is thought that the courts would not order such a procedure to be carried out. While courts in other jurisdictions have sanctioned Caesarean deliveries in the face of maternal opposition (*Re S (adult: refusal of medical treatment)* (1992) (England); *Jefferson Griffin Spalding County Hospital Authority* (1981) (USA)), the tide appears to have turned against such an invasive approach (*St George's Healthcare National Health Service Trust v. S (No. 2)*; *R v. Collins, ex p. S* (England); *Baby Boy Doe v. Mother Doe* (1994) (USA)).

The ante-natal period may be relevant for the purpose of criminal law. So, for example, while, as a general rule, murder and culpable homicide can only be committed in respect of a living person, a charge of murder is competent where the child is still partially inside the mother's body (*H.M. Advocate v. Scott* (1892)). Destruction of a non-viable foetus in the womb will normally amount to abortion and, unless performed within the permitted parameters, will constitute an offence. Where injury is inflicted on the foetus or pregnant woman and the child, subsequently born alive, dies as a result of these injuries, criminal responsibility will attach. Thus, the driver of a car which collided with another vehicle in which a pregnant woman was the passenger was convicted of causing death by reckless driving, when the baby died the following day as a result of injuries sustained in the collision (*McCluskey v. H.M. Advocate* (1989)).

Abortion
Prior to 1967, legally-sanctioned abortion was not generally available in Scotland. Since the passing of the Abortion Act 1967, it is no longer an offence to procure or participate in an abortion in certain circumstances. The 1967 Act has been amended fairly extensively by the Human Fertilisation and Embryology Act 1990. No offence is committed where the abortion is performed by a registered medical practitioner and in a National Health Service hospital or place approved by the Secretary of State, provided that at least one of the conditions set out in section 1(1) of the 1967 Act is satisfied. The conditions are:

(a) Two registered medical practitioners must have formed the opinion in good faith that *continuation of the pregnancy would involve greater risk to the physical or mental health of the woman or any existing children in her family than would a termination.* Such a termination is only permitted up to the twenty-fourth week of pregnancy.
(b) The termination is necessary to prevent *grave permanent injury to the physical or mental health of the pregnant woman.* Terminations under this condition may be authorised by a single practitioner and are not subject to any time limit.
(c) *Continuation of the pregnancy would involve risk to life of the pregnant woman greater than termination.* Again, terminations under this condition may be authorised by a single practitioner and are not subject to any time limit.
(d) Two registered medical practitioners have formed the opinion in good faith that there is *substantial risk that if the child was born alive it would suffer from such physical or mental abnormalities as to be seriously handicapped.* Again, this condition is not subject to any time limit.

Some health care professionals have a conscientious objection to abortion and section 4 of the 1967 Act excuses them from participating in an abortion unless the treatment is directed at saving the life or health of the pregnant woman.

The decision to seek a termination lies, at first instance, with the pregnant woman, who must fulfill one of the conditions outlined above. It is well-established in other jurisdictions that the potential father has no standing to prevent the abortion from taking place

(*Paton v. Trustees of BPAS* (1979) (England); *C v. S* (England); *Tremblay v. Daigle* (1989) (Canada)). Surprisingly, it was not until 1997 that the Scottish courts had the opportunity to consider the matter for the first time. In *Kelly v. Kelly* (1997), the husband of a pregnant woman sought interdict to prevent his wife having a termination. Given the clear indication from abroad that a husband has no standing to prevent an abortion proceeding, the case was argued on a different, rather ingenious, basis. For Mr Kelly it was argued that a child can claim damages for antenatal injury on the basis of the *nasciturus* principle, that such claims could be made by the child's guardian, that interdict was competent to prevent a wrong occurring, and that he was therefore entitled to seek interdict in the present circumstances (as the potential child's guardian). The Second Division rejected his claim on the basis that, while a living child had a right of action in respect of injuries sustained in the womb, the foetus has no legal personality and, thus, can have no rights which are capable of being protected by interdict. In particular, the court took the view that Scots law confers no right on the foetus to a continued existence in the womb, since such a right would conflict with the woman's right to seek a termination under the 1967 Act. An aggrieved husband in Mr Kelly's situation would almost certainly have grounds for an action of divorce on the basis that his wife's behaviour, in having a termination against his wishes, made it unreasonable to expect him to continue to live with her (Divorce (Scotland) Act 1976, s. 1(2)(b)).

Wrongful birth or conception
Some adults decide either that they do not want to have children at all or that their existing family is large enough. They view a sterilisation operation (female) or a vasectomy (male) as a more certain option than simply relying on contraception. Where the operation is unsuccessful and pregnancy follows, the couple (or single person) may consider an action in delict against the hospital involved. Two distinct causes of action may arise. First, there is the possibility that the operation itself was performed negligently. Secondly, while the operation may have been performed with reasonable care, the health care professionals involved may have been negligent in failing to advise the couple of the possibility that the operation would not be a success and the advisability of using contraception until the success or otherwise of the operation could be established.

After initial reluctance (*Udale v. Bloomsbury Area Health Authority* (1983)), courts in England accepted that, in either situation, the parents of the unplanned child had the right to recover damages in respect not only of the mother's pain and suffering but also for the very substantial costs associated with raising a child (*Emeh v. Kensington and Chelsea and Westminster Area Health Authority* (1985)). Yet again, it was some time before the Scottish courts had the opportunity to consider the issue and it was thought that the position here was the same as that arrived at in England. In 1997, the whole question returned to centre-stage with two conflicting Outer House decisions (*McFarlane v. Tayside Health Board* (1997) and *Anderson v. Forth Valley Health Board* (1998)), before the Inner House was able to clarify matters (*McFarlane v. Tayside Health Board* (1998)). The result is that Scots law does, indeed, permit recovery in respect of the birth of a healthy baby, where the requisite negligence precedes the birth.

Where a child is born with disabilities that could have been foreseen in the circumstances, and the parents were not warned, they have an action in delict against whoever failed to inform them of the risk, their measure of damages being the additional cost of raising the child (*McLelland v. Greater Glasgow Health Board* (1998)). Essentially, by not being informed of the likely dangers, the pregnant woman (and to some extent her partner) has been deprived of the opportunity to seek a termination. This claim by the child's parents should be distinguished from the child's claim for "wrongful life".

Wrongful life
Attempts by the child to recover damages in respect of his or her disabilities have proved almost universally unsuccessful, where the child attempts to argue that, had the likelihood of his or her condition been known, he or she would either not have been conceived or would have been aborted while a foetus. Essentially, the child is really arguing that, had all the relevant facts been known, he or she would not have been born at all. With few exceptions (*Curlender v. Bio-Science Laboratories* (1980)), the courts in the USA have rejected such actions on the basis that they are unwilling to take the view that no life at all would be preferable to life with disabilities, that the measure of damages is impossible to assess, and judicial antipathy towards what might be perceived as promoting abortion (*Gleitman v. Cosgrove* (1967); *Ellis v. Sherman* (1986); *Crowe v. Forum Group Inc.* (1991)). The only English case on the point rejected the child's claim on the same grounds (*McKay v. Essex Area Health Authority* (1982)) and such actions may now be precluded by statute there (Congenital Disabilities (Civil Liability) Act 1976, s. 1(2)(b)). While the Scottish Law Commission was unwilling to commit itself on the matter (*Report on Liability for Antenatal Injury* (1973)), the courts here have now rejected one such claim, at least in the context of compensation for criminal injury (*P's Curator Bonis v. Criminal Injuries Compensation Board* (1997)).

THE END OF LEGAL PERSONALITY

Death
Essentially, legal personality ends at death. The dilemmas surrounding the end of a person's life and, particularly, any medical involvement in that process, attract sincere, strongly-held opinions, which are as polarised as those surrounding the abortion debate. At the outset,

it may be helpful to draw a distinction between withdrawal of medical treatment from a patient (*i.e.* doing little or nothing) and assisting suicide (*i.e.* doing something to promote a person's death).

Withdrawal of medical treatment
Where a competent, adult patient requests the withdrawal of medical treatment, or requests that treatment should be confined to a specific limited type (*e.g.* relief of pain), there is no legal problem. Treatment of an adult against his or her wishes normally constitutes an assault and, once the patient's views are known, they must be respected. Where the patient is no longer competent, the decision on treatment must be made by someone else. The paradigm case of an incompetent patient is one who is in a permanent vegetative state (PVS).

Until the decision in *Law Hospital NHS Trust v. Lord Advocate* (1996) and directions from the Lord Advocate clarified matters, the families and doctors of such patients were in an uncertain legal position when considering how to proceed. In that case, the patient had been in PVS for over four years. The pursuers sought declarator that it would not be unlawful for them to discontinue all life-sustaining and medical treatments and to provide only such treatments as would allow her to die peacefully. The Inner House concluded the test in such cases was what would serve the "best interests" of the patient. It explained further that the "best interests" test should be, "viewed negatively, namely, that it is not in the best interests of the patient to be kept alive by artificial means, where the court is satisfied that the diagnosis is so clear and the prognosis so futile that the [patient] has no interest in being kept alive" (at p.517). The case was remitted back to the Lord Ordinary, who pronounced declarator and the patient subsequently died. Of course, that case was relevant only to civil liability. In order to avoid continuing uncertainty with regard to criminal liability, the Lord Advocate issued a policy statement indicating that he would not authorise prosecution of a medical practitioner who withdrew treatment from a patient in PVS provided that the action was taken in good faith and with the authority of the court.

While the courts have shown themselves willing to consider evidence of "what the patient would have wanted", at present there is nothing an individual can do in advance to determine what will happen. The Scottish Law Commission considered empowering people to make arrangements for the future through the mechanism of "advance statements" (better known as "living wills"). It recommended that such statements should be valid, subject to exceptions and the possibility of revocation (*Report on Incapable Adults* (1995), paras 5.41–5.59).

Assisted suicide and euthanasia
There have been a number of attempts to legalise physician-assisted suicide in other jurisdictions but, to date, most have had no long-term success. A notable exception is the provision for assisted suicide in the

Death with Dignity Act, which has been operating in Oregon, USA, since 1998. The Act requires the physician and the patient to comply with a number of, fairly rigorous, conditions before the physician can prescribe a lethal prescription of drugs for the patient to take.

In Scotland, assisted suicide, regardless of whether the assistance is given by a doctor or someone else, is illegal. Depending on the circumstances, the accused may be chaiged with murder or culpable homicide and it may be some reflection of the attitude of prosecutors that, even where the original charge is murder, the accused's guilty plea to the lesser charge is often accepted (*H. M. Advocate v. Brady* (1997)). In addition, there are cases which illustrate leniency in sentencing where it is accepted that the accused acted out of concern for the deceased in killing him or her. However, such decisions are no guarantee that a particular prosecutor or court would take an equally compassionate and lenient attitude in the future.

Presumption of death
Sometimes, while all the circumstances point to the fact that a person has died, no body can be produced. For example, where a person boarded an aeroplane which crashed into the ocean with no survivors, it is reasonable to presume that the person has died. In addition, the law accepts less dramatic circumstances as indicating death, as for example where a person has been missing for a long period of time and no one comes forward to indicate that the person is alive. The matter has long been regulated by statute and the current statute is the Presumption of Death (Scotland) Act 1977. An action to have a person declared dead may be brought in either the sheriff court or the Court of Session by any person having an interest (s. 1(1)). A declarator is competent in two situations. The first arises where there is a clear indication that a person died at a particular time, as in the case of the passenger on the crashed aeroplane, and the action can be raised immediately after the crash. The second situation arises where the person "has not been known to be alive for a period of at least seven years" and, obviously, such actions may only be raised after that period of time has elapsed. Where it is established that either of the two conditions is satisfied, the court must grant the declarator providing that the person died, in the first case, at a specific date or, in the second case, at the date seven years after the person was last known to be alive.

Once a person has been declared dead, the decree is conclusive on all matters and effective against any person for all civil purposes including any rights in property (s. 3). Such a decree terminates the missing person's marriage for all time and the limited provisions allowing for variation or recall of the decree do not revive the marriage (s. 4(5)). Only criminal liability is unaffected by a declarator of death. In order to accommodate the possibility that the person declared dead might reappear, the Act contains provision for variation or recall of the decree (s. 4). Where the missing person reappears within five years, the court can make such order as is "fair and reasonable in all the circumstances of the case" regulating property rights, but such orders do not affect any rights acquired by a third party in good faith and for value (s. 5).

Presumption of survivorship
Where two people die in a common calamity, it may be impossible to ascertain which of them survived the other and the Succession (Scotland) Act 1964 introduced a general presumption that the younger person survives the elder (s. 31(1)(b)). However, there are two exceptions to this presumption. First, where the two persons were husband and wife, neither is presumed to survive the other (s. 31(1)(a)). This prevents the estates of both of them being inherited by the survivors of only one. The second exception applies where the elder person has left property to the younger, whom failing to a third party. Where the younger person has died intestate, the elder person is presumed to have survived the younger (for the purpose of that particular legacy only) and the property passes to the third party (s. 32). The whole scheme introduced by the 1964 Act applies only in cases of doubt and if it can be established, on the balance of probabilities, that one person did in fact survive the other, then the usual rules of succession apply (*Lamb v. H. M. Advocate* (1976)). For this reason, it is quite common in wills for the testator to provide that a particular beneficiary will only inherit if he or she survives the testator by, for example, 30 days. This ensures that either the beneficiary will enjoy the property or that it will pass to other people chosen by the testator.

Further reading
J. K. Mason and R. A. McCall Smith, *Law and Medical Ethics* (5th ed., 1999, Butterworths), chaps 5, 6, 7, 13, 16 and 17
E. E. Sutherland, *Child and Family Law* (T & T Clark, 1999), chap. 2
A. B. Wilkinson and K. McK. Norrie, *The Law of Parent and Child in Scotland* (2nd ed., W. Green, 1999), chap. 2

---

3. CHILDREN, PARENTS AND OTHER FAMILY MEMBERS

The second half of the twentieth century has seen enormous changes in the way the legal system views children, both in their own right and as family members. In this chapter, we will examine the emergence of the concept of children's rights and the significance of a child's age, before moving on to look at the way children are regarded as being linked to significant adults, through biological parenthood or the fictions applying to assisted reproduction.

CHILDREN'S RIGHTS

Internationally, children can benefit from rights given to all persons, irrespective of age, and such instruments as the European Convention on Human Rights (1950) apply to them. The importance of this Convention will increase with the passing of the Human Rights Act 1998. The high point in international recognition of children's rights came in 1989 when the Convention on the Rights of the Child was adopted unanimously by the General Assembly of the United Nations. The United Kingdom ratified the Convention in 1991 and there is no doubt that its provisions influenced subsequent legislation here and, in particular, the Children (Scotland) Act 1995. We will examine the Act in more detail in later chapters. However, it is important at this point to be aware of the Act's overarching principles, sometimes described as the child lawyer's mantra. They are:

(a) The welfare of the child is the paramount consideration;
(b) The child must be given the opportunity to express his or her views and account will be taken of these views in the light of the child's age and maturity;
(c) The court will not make any order unless to do so will be better than making no order at all.

THE SIGNIFICANCE OF AGE

As we have seen, every child acquires legal personality from the moment of birth. However, there are obvious practical reasons why young children cannot be active participants in the legal system. Thus, the law has always recognised that a child cannot acquire legal capacity until a later stage. Since maturity is a very individual matter, the legal system sometimes prefers to link capacity to the readily verifiable fact of chronological age. Age is calculated by regarding a person as reaching a particular age at the beginning of the relevant anniversary of his or her birth (Age of Legal Capacity (Scotland) Act 1991, s. 6(1)), *i.e.* just after midnight on one's birthday. Where a person is born on February 29, the relevant anniversary is March 1 in any year other than a leap year (1991 Act, s. 6(2)).

The general rule is that *a person below the age of 16* has *no legal capacity* to enter into transactions and that any attempt to do so is void (1991 Act, s. 1(1)). If the law left it at that, we would be in the absurd position that a 12-year-old could not enter a contract to buy a bar of chocolate. For this reason, there are a host of exceptions to this general rule and the exceptions are often more important than the rule itself. The exceptions are contained in the 1991 Act and are as follows:

(a) *Common transactions.* Children have the capacity to enter a transaction provided that two conditions are satisfied. First, the transaction itself must be of a kind commonly entered into by persons of the child's age and circumstances and, secondly, the terms of the transaction must not be unreasonable (s. 2(1)). This is the most flexible and practically significant of the exceptions to the general rule.

(b) *Instructing a solicitor in connection with a civil matter.* A person under the age of 16 has the capacity to instruct a solicitor in connection with a civil matter provided that the child or young person has a general understanding of what it means to do so (s. 2(4A)). A child of 12 years or older is presumed to have sufficient understanding, although younger children may qualify. None of this has any bearing on the child's capacity in relation to any criminal matter (s. 2(4)(c)).

(c) *Making a will.* A young person of 12 years old or over has the capacity to make a will (s. 2(2)).

(d) *Consenting to adoption.* A young person of 12 years old or over has the right to consent to or veto his or her own adoption (s. 2(3)).

(e) *Consenting to surgical, dental or medical treatment.* A person below the age of 16 has the capacity to consent to any surgical, medical or dental procedure or treatment where the qualified practitioner attending him or her is of the opinion that the young person understands the nature and possible consequences of the procedure or treatment (s. 2(4)).

(f) *Transactions entered into before the commencement of the Act.* Where the transaction was entered into before the Act came into force on September 25, 1991, the common law rules will apply (s. 1(3)(a)).

(g) *Parental responsibilities and rights.* While parental responsibilities and rights are usually held in respect of a person under 16, such young people may themselves be parents. Where this happens, the young parent may hold parental responsibilities and rights in respect of his or her own child (s. 1(3)(g)).

(h) *Other matters not affected.* While the 1991 Act supersedes all prior legislation governing the capacity of young people (s. 1(4)), it makes clear that its provisions do not affect certain other matters. Thus, legislation laying down age limits expressed in years remains valid (s. 1(3)(d)). Delictual liability and criminal responsibility remain unaffected by the Act (s. 1(3)(c)).

Young people *over the age of 16* have *full legal capacity* to enter into any transaction (s. 1(1)(b)). However, the 1991 Act recognises that these "beginners", in terms of exercising capacity, may need some additional protection from their own inexperience and greater vulnerability to exploitation. It allows a person under the age of 21 to apply to the court to have a transaction which he or she entered into while between the ages of 16 and 18 set aside (s. 3(1)). In order to mount a successful challenge, the young person must demonstrate that the transaction was a "prejudicial transaction", defined in terms of two criteria. First, it must be shown that the transaction was one which an adult, exercising reasonable prudence, would not have entered into in the circumstances at the time (s. 3(2)(a)). Secondly, it must be shown that the transaction itself has caused, or is likely to cause, substantial prejudice to the young person (s. 3(2)(b)).

Regardless of their impact on the young person, certain transactions and other activities are explicitly exempted from applications for reduction under the Act. It should be remembered that this does not bar applications for reduction on the many other grounds available to anyone, irrespective of age, including misrepresentation, fraud, and coercion. The following cannot be challenged under the 1991 Act:

(a)   making a will;
(b)   consent to adoption;
(c)   action taken in the course of civil proceedings;
(d)   consent to any surgical, medical or dental procedure;
(e)   a transaction entered into by the young person in the course of his or her trade, occupation or profession;
(f)   a transaction where a young person has induced the other party to enter it by fraudulent misrepresentation as to his or her age or any other material fact;
(g)   a transaction which the young person has ratified after reaching the age of 18, knowing that it could be set aside;
(h)   a transaction which has been given prior approval by a court on the application of all of the parties to it, including the young person (s. 3(3)).

Age in other contexts

The 1991 Act specifically excludes delict and the criminal law from its ambit, nor does it affect age-related restrictions found in other statutes (s. 1(3)). A child can claim damages in delict from any age and the child's parents are not placed in any special position, in this respect, since a child can sue his or her parents (*Young v. Rankin* (1934)).The fact that a pursuer in an action founded on delict is a child does become relevant, however, in the context of contributory negligence; that is, when the defender argues that the harm was caused, at least in part, by the child's own conduct. The child's behaviour here is assessed in the light of that child's age and experience and, thus, a child of five, living in an urban environment, can be expected to have some appreciation of the dangers of traffic (*McKinnell v. White* (1971)). There is no minimum age for delictual liability in Scotland. Where the parent instigates the child's delictual act or has been negligent in, for example, failing to supervise the child, liability may attach to the parent. However, parents have no automatic responsibility for the delictual acts of their children.

Scots law attributes criminal responsibility from the age of eight years old and Scotland has one of the lowest ages for criminal responsibility in the world. Where a child is alleged to have committed an offence, he or she will almost always be dealt with in the children's hearing system which adopts a treatment-based approach to the child's problems (see chapter 7). However, prosecution of children in the criminal courts is provided for in a limited range of circumstances, on the instructions of the Lord Advocate (Criminal Procedure (Scotland) Act 1995, s. 42). Where convicted, the child can be sentenced by the court, although provision is made for involving the children's hearing system in sentencing. This involvement does not apply to cases where the penalty for the case is fixed by law and, thus, a child convicted of murder will not benefit from the provision.

An enormous number of age-related restrictions exist. Since they were introduced at different times and, sometimes, as a quick response to a particular burning issue of the day, they are inconsistent. The rationale behind age-related restrictions is often to protect children from perceived dangers of the adult world. Thus, the attempt is made to deny children below a particular age access to tobacco (16 years), alcohol (16/18) and gambling (16/18). Sometimes the desire is to protect the community as well as children, hence restrictions on driving (16–21) and possessing air-rifles and firearms (14–17). On other occasions, the law appears to be offering guidance on what might be described as "good parenting". This would explain legislation which prohibits giving alcohol to a child below the age of five, except for medical purposes.

PARENTAGE

As we shall see, the fact of being a child's parent may be important for a whole range of purposes. Mothers and married fathers acquire automatic parental responsibilities and rights. Parental consent is normally required before a child can be adopted. Thus, establishing the child-parent link is important. In addition, sight should not be lost of the social and psychological importance of knowing about parentage as part of one's identity. Of course, in most cases, the matter is uncontentious. We will look first at parentage in the "traditional" setting before moving on to reproductive technology and its implications for parentage.

Maternity
Disputes over the maternity of a child are rare, although not unknown, as evidenced by *Douglas v. Duke of Hamilton* (1769). Maternity may be important for immigration purposes and the advent of DNA profiling has been of assistance in resolving disputed cases in this context. Cases have arisen in other jurisdictions where it has been alleged that, due to an error at the hospital, two women have gone home with each other's baby, the mistake being discovered at a later stage (*Twigg v. Mays* (1989 and 1993) (USA)), with the resulting

dispute being over both the maternity and the paternity of the children.

Paternity

Paternity disputes have long been a feature of the legal system and section 5 of the Law Reform (Parent and Child) (Scotland) Act 1986 contains a number of presumptions to assist the courts in disputed cases. These presumptions merely provide a legal starting point and all of them are rebuttable; that is, they can be displaced by proof on the balance of probabilities (s. 5(4)). A man is presumed to be the father of a child in the following circumstances:

(a) *if he was married to the child's mother at any time from the child's conception to his or her birth* (s. 5(1)(a)). This presumption applies to all kinds of marriage and regular, irregular, void and voidable marriages are all sufficient to trigger its application (s. 5(2));

(b) *where the above provision does not apply, if both he and the mother have acknowledged that he is the father and he has been registered as such* (s. 5(1)(b));

(c) *where the court has declared him to be the father of a child* (s. 5(3)). As we will see, the court can grant declarator of parentage; that is, it can declare that a particular man is a child's father. Such a declarator will be presumed to be accurate unless displaced by a later successful challenge.

Establishing parentage or non-parentage

While disputes over a child's parentage are almost always about paternity, rather than maternity, the same procedure applies in either case. An action for declarator of parentage or non-parentage may be raised in either the Court of Session or the sheriff court (1986 Act, s. 7(1)) and parentage may also be determined incidentally to other proceedings (s. 7(5)). The action may be raised by anyone with an interest, including, of course, the child, although most actions are raised by mothers seeking to establish paternity. In order to rebut any of the presumptions discussed above, the pursuer must prove his or her case on the balance of probabilities (1986 Act, s. 5(4)). The court must be satisfied as to the sufficiency of evidence (Civil Evidence (Scotland) Act 1988, s. 8(1)), but corroborated evidence is no longer required (1988 Act, s. 1(1)).

The most popular evidence led relies on DNA profiling, which makes it possible to establish that a person *is* the father of a child. Since DNA profiling requires the taking of a sample of blood or other body tissue from the parties involved, it raises the issue of consent to testing. While a civil court cannot compel a competent adult to submit to such a test (*Whitehall v. Whitehall* (1958); *Torrie v. Turner* (1990)), the court may request a party to the proceedings to do so and draw any contrary inference from refusal as it considers appropriate (Law Reform

(Miscellaneous (Provisions) (Scotland) Act 1990, s. 70). This does not mean that the pursuer will automatically succeed in establishing paternity (*Smith v. Greenhill* (1994)), but it does reduce the incentive simply to keep one's head down. A sample will also be required from the child. Where he or she is of sufficient age and understanding to appreciate what is involved in the test and the likely consequences, he or she can consent (Age of Legal Capacity (Scotland) Act 1991, s. 2(4)), but, in most cases, children are too young to give consent. Any person who has parental responsibilities in respect of the child under 16 or care and control of him or her may consent on the child's behalf (1986 Act, s. 6(2)). The court can consent to samples being taken from "any person who is incapable of giving consent" in two situations (1986 Act, s. 6(3)). The first is where there is no one entitled to give consent and the second is where there is a person with capacity to consent but either it is not reasonably practicable to obtain that person's consent, or that person is unwilling to accept the responsibility of giving or withholding consent. The court is prohibited from consenting to the taking of a sample unless it is satisfied that the taking of the sample "would not be detrimental to the person's health" (1986 Act, s. 6(4)).

Where the samples necessary for DNA profiling cannot be obtained, other forms of evidence will be relevant. For example, evidence of an established relationship between the child's mother and the alleged father might support establishing his paternity, while evidence of the gestation period (the time between conception and birth) was usually used to suggest that a particular man was not the father of the child. Evidence of a physical resemblance between the child and the alleged father is not generally accepted by courts (*S v. S* (1977); *cf. Grant v. Countess of Seafield* (1926)).

ASSISTED REPRODUCTION

Enormous scientific advances have been made in the field of assisted reproduction and individuals and couples who are experiencing difficulty in having a child can now be helped through a range of treatment options. The *Report of the Committee of Inquiry into Human Fertilisation and Embryology* (1984) attempted to address the ethical and legal dilemmas surrounding the techniques. It resulted in the Human Fertilisation and Embryology Act 1990 which provides for the regulation of fertility services, usually through the Human Fertilisation and Embryology Authority (HFEA), and for rules on determining parentage. We will look briefly at the techniques available before considering the rules on parentage which apply to children who result from them.

The techniques
Donor insemination (D.I.)
D.I. is the process whereby semen obtained from a (usually anonymous) donor is injected into the woman's uterus. If fertilisation

occurs, the resulting pregnancy proceeds in the usual way. For a married or cohabiting couple who are experiencing difficulty in having a child due to the male partner's infertility, donor insemination is a relatively simple way for them to have a child who is biologically linked to the woman. It should be noted that donor insemination does not constitute adultery for the purpose of divorce (*McLennan v. McLennan* (1958)). Were a wife to undergo donor insemination without her husband's consent, her distressed husband could probably obtain a divorce on the basis that her action made it unreasonable to expect him to live with her (Divorce (Scotland) Act 1976, s. 1(2)(b)). Whether donor insemination ought to be provided to unmarried couples or single women is a controversial issue.

Partner insemination (P.I.)
The technique for P.I. is the same as that for D.I., save that the donor is the woman's partner. Controversy surrounded the decision of the Court of Appeal in *R. v. Human Fertilisation and Embryology Authority, ex p. Blood* (1997), where a widow was successful in gaining permission to use her deceased husband's semen and, ultimately, had their child. The semen had been removed while he was in a coma and, since he had no opportunity to give his consent to its use after his death, the 1990 Act prevented such use in the United Kingdom (Sched. 3, para. 2(2)). However, the court felt bound by European law to permit its export to Belgium where the widow obtained treatment. The case prompted a further review of the law (*Review of the Consent Provisions of the Human Fertilisation and Embryology Act 1990* (1998)) and further legislation may result.

In vitro fertilisation (IVF)
IVF involves the fertilisation of the ovum in laboratory conditions and the transfer of the resulting embryo into the uterus. The ovum may have come from the woman into whom the embryo is implanted or from a donor. The fertilising sperm may have come from her partner, if she has one, or a donor.

Surrogacy
There are a large number of different arrangements which can lead to what is described as "surrogacy". What is known as "full surrogacy" involves a woman ("the surrogate") agreeing to carry a foetus, produced from the gametes (sperm and ovum) obtained from a couple ("the commissioning couple"), with the intention that the child will be handed over to the couple to be raised by them as their child. "Partial surrogacy" may involve sperm donated by the husband of the commissioning couple being used to fertilise the surrogate's own ovum. Surrogacy has attracted more controversy than other techniques used to assist in reproduction, partly because of the greater degree of active involvement of a third party, and partly because of the commercialism associated with it. The Surrogacy Arrangements

Act 1985 was passed to address the second concern. It makes it an offence to negotiate a surrogacy arrangement on a commercial basis (ss. 1(8) and 2(3)) or to be involved in advertising such arrangements (s. 3) and renders surrogacy agreements unenforceable (s. 1A). Surrogacy has been the subject of further review and future legislation may result in surrogates being entitled to receive limited expenses only (*Surrogacy Review for Health Ministers of Current Arrangements for Payments and Regulation* (1998)).

Parentage

The 1990 Act provides a number of rules on the parentage of children produced as a result of assisted reproduction. It should be noted that these are fixed rules and, unlike the presumptions of paternity, discussed above, cannot be rebutted. Where a person is to be treated as the mother or father of a child as a result of the Act, the effect is stated to apply "for all purposes" (s. 29(1)), although it does not apply to the transmission of any title, coat of arms, honour or dignity (s. 29(5)(a)). While references in enactments, deeds and other instruments are to be construed as if a child-parent relationship existed (s. 29(3)), it is open to any person executing a deed to provide that this is not to be the effect.

Maternity

Where a woman is carrying, or has carried, a child as a result of an embryo or sperm and eggs being placed in her, that woman and no other woman is to be treated as the mother of the child (s. 27(1)). There are two ways by which the carrying woman can be displaced as the child's mother. The first is where the child is adopted by the ordinary method of adoption whereby the adopters take over as the child's parents and the child's legal link with birth relatives is severed (s. 27(3)). The second is through the special provision, introduced by the 1990 Act and confined to surrogacy, whereby the couple who commissioned a surrogate to carry a foetus, genetically linked to one or both of the couple, can apply for a special kind of parental order (s. 30). This parental order is, effectively, a form of accelerated adoption and is discussed below.

Paternity

The provision dealing with paternity is a little more complicated than that on maternity. It applies not only where a child is being or has been carried by a woman as a result of an embryo, or sperm and eggs being placed in her, but also where the woman has been inseminated artificially (s. 28(1)). Where the woman was married at the time of the treatment but the embryo was created using sperm from someone other than her husband, her husband is treated as the child's father unless it can be shown that he did not agree to the treatment (s. 28(2)). Thus, the onus is placed firmly on the husband to rebut consent. Where no man would be treated as the child's father by the application of the provision dealing with husbands, discussed above, the woman's partner will be treated as the child's father, provided that *both* of the following conditions are met:

- the man and woman are treated together;
- in the course of treatment services are provided by a person who is licensed to provide such services (s. 28(3)).

Parental orders

Mention has been made of the special provision for the making of a parental order in favour of gametes donors, essentially an order which is similar to an adoption order (1990 Act, s. 30). Such an order is available only where a host of conditions are satisfied and is, in any event, at the discretion of the court. The conditions are as follows:

(a) the application must be made by a married couple;
(b) the child concerned must have been carried by a woman other than the wife as a result of the placing in her of an embryo or sperm and eggs or her artificial insemination;
(c) the gametes of the husband or the wife, or both, were used to bring about the creation of the embryo;
(d) the couple must apply for the order within six months of the child's birth;
(e) the child's home must be with the couple both at the time of the application and at the time of the order being made;
(f) the husband or the wife, or both, must be domiciled in the United Kingdom or in the Channel Islands or the Isle of Man at the time of the application and at the time of the order being made;
(g) both the husband and the wife must have attained the age of 18 by the time any order is made;
(h) both the woman who carried the child and the father of the child (including a man treated as such by virtue of section 28 of the Act) have freely, and with full understanding of what is involved, agreed unconditionally to the making of the order;
(i) the court must be satisfied that no money or other benefit (other than for expenses reasonably incurred) has been given or received by the husband or the wife for: the making of the order, any agreement required, the handing over of the child to them, or the making of any arrangements with a view to the making of the order.

Further reading
A. Cleland and E. E. Sutherland (eds), *Children's Rights in Scotland* (1996, W. Green)
J. K. Mason, *Medico-Legal Aspects of Reproduction and Parenthood* (1998, Dartmouth)
J. K. Mason and R. A. McCall Smith, *Law and Medical Ethics* (5th ed., 1999, Butterworths), chaps 3 and 10

E. E. Sutherland, *Child and Family Law* (T & T Clark, 1999), chaps 3
    and 4
A. B. Wilkinson and K. McK. Norrie, *The Law of Parent and Child
    in Scotland* (2nd ed., W. Green, 1999), chaps 3, 6, 7 and 15

---

4. ADOPTION

Adoption is the creation of the child-parent relationship by order of
the court. The concept came to Scots law comparatively late, in 1930.
Typically, it provided for a single mother, who felt unable to raise her
child, handing the child over, via an agency, to a married couple. The
adoption setting has changed dramatically since the early days. Few
adoptions now involve babies and more older children are being
adopted. Almost half of all adoptions are step-parent adoptions; that
is, adoption by a parent's new husband or wife, with the child living
with the parent and new spouse. The current law on adoption is found
in the Adoption (Scotland) Act 1978 and references are to that Act,
as amended, unless otherwise stated.

THE PURPOSE OF MODERN ADOPTION LAW

Whatever benefits adoption may bring to the adults involved, the
child's interests are the focal point of adoption and the overarching
principles apply.

Paramouncy of the child's welfare
The court or adoption agency is directed to "regard the need to safeguard and promote *the welfare of the child* throughout his [or her] life
as the paramount consideration" (s. 6(1)(a), emphasis added). In
assessing welfare, regard should be had to the child's "religious per-
suasion, racial origin and cultural and linguistic background" (s.
6(1)(b)(ii)).

The child's views
In assessing welfare, regard shall also be had "to *the child's views* (if
he [or she] wishes to express them) taking account of his [or her] age
and maturity" (s. 6(1)(b)(i), emphasis added). In addition, a child of
12 years old and over has the right to veto or consent to his or her
own adoption (Age of Legal Capacity (Scotland) Act 1991, s. 2(3)).

Presumed non-intervention
The adoption agency is obliged to consider whether "there is some
better, practicable, alternative" to adoption before it makes any adoption arrangements (s. 6A). The court is directed not to make an adop-

tion order, or an order freeing a child for adoption, "unless it considers that it would be better for the child that it should do so than that it should not" (s. 24(3)).

THE PARTIES INVOLVED IN ADOPTION

Who may be adopted?
Any person under the age of 18 who has never been married may be adopted (s. 12(1) and (5)), and an adopted child may be the subject of a subsequent adoption order (s. 12(7)). Provided that the proceedings began before the child's eighteenth birthday, the petition can be granted after he or she reaches 18 (s. 12(1)).

Who may adopt?
The 1978 Act makes provision for adoption by married (by definition heterosexual) couples or single people. As we saw in chapter 3, there are a host of special requirements for the expedited adoptions which apply in some surrogacy cases. In the ordinary case, adopters must satisfy a number of requirements. Applicants must be at least 21 years old (ss. 14(1) and 15(1)) unless the applicant is the child's parent, in which case the age is 18. Where two people apply to adopt a child together, they must be married to each other (s. 14(1)). A sole applicant for adoption must satisfy the court either that he or she is unmarried (s. 15(1)(a)); or, if married, that it is a step-parent adoption (see below); or that his or her spouse cannot be found; or that the couple have separated permanently; or that his or her spouse is incapable, by reason of ill-health (whether physical or mental) of making an application for an adoption order (s. 15(1)(b)). In the case of a couple, one party must be domiciled in a part of the United Kingdom, the Channel Islands or the Isle of Man (s. 12(2)(a)) or the couple must have been resident in one of these places for at least a year immediately prior to their application (s. 14(2)(c)). A similar requirement applies to single applicants (s. 15(2)). The requirement of domicile or residence does not apply to adoptions under the Hague Convention (s. 14(2)(b)).

Step-parent adoption
The increase in step-families has resulted in an increase in step-parent adoption. The step-parent applying to adopt must satisfy the general requirements for adoption outlined above. A difficulty with step-parent adoptions has always been that, once the adoption takes place, it severs the child's legal link with the "other" birth parent (*i.e.* the birth parent who is not married to the step-parent) and that parent's relatives. Where the "other" parent is opposed to the step-parent's adoption of a child, the court may dispense with that parent's consent, but it will not do so lightly (*A v. B* (1987) and *AB and CD v. EF* (1991)). If the adoption order is granted, the parent to whom the step-parent is married retains his or her original status, with all the parental responsibilities that he or she had prior to the adoption (ss. 12(3A) and 39(1)).

THE AGREEMENT OF THE CHILD'S PARENTS AND GUARDIANS

Parents and guardians

The starting point in adoption is that *each* parent and guardian of the child must freely, and with full understanding of what is involved, agree unconditionally to the making of the adoption order (s. 16(1)). The consent of the child's mother is ineffective if given less than six weeks after the child's birth (s. 16(4)). "Guardian" means "a person appointed by deed or will or by a court of competent jurisdiction to be the guardian of the child" (s. 65(1)). "Parent", for this purpose, means *only* the following persons:

(a)   the mother of the child, where she has parental responsibilities or rights in relation to him or her;
(b)   the father of the child, where he has parental responsibilities or rights in relation to him or her;
(c)   both parents where they both have parental responsibilities or rights (s. 65(1)).

The unmarried father

It is only if the unmarried father has any of the parental responsibilities or rights, whether by agreement with the child's mother or by court order, that his consent to adoption is required. However, before a court may make an order freeing a child for adoption, it must be satisfied, in respect of any person claiming to be the child's father: that he does not intend to apply for an order in respect of parental responsibilities or rights; that if he did apply, it is likely that the order would be refused; that he has no intention of entering into a parental responsibilities and rights agreement with the child's mother; and, regardless of his intention, that such an agreement is unlikely to result (1978 Act, s. 18(7)).

DISPENSING WITH PARENTAL AGREEMENT

While parental consent to adoption is central to respect for family integrity, there are circumstances where the parents are unable or wholly unsuited to fulfil any active role as parents. Thus, there is provision for dispensing with parental consent to adoption. This involves a two-stage process (s. 16(1)(b)). (See, *P v. Lothian Regional Council* (1989) and *L v. Central Regional Council* (1990).) First, it must be established, as a matter of fact, that one of the four grounds for dispensing with parental consent exists. Only then is the court in a position to move to the second stage—deciding whether it *should* make such a dispensation. As with all decisions in the adoption, the court must decide this second stage by applying the welfare test. The grounds for dispensing with parental consent are found in section 16(2) and are as follows:

(a) *The parent or guardian is not known, cannot be found or is incapable of giving agreement.* It will be very rare that the identity of a child's mother is not known but, occasionally, babies are abandoned and the mother is never traced. Before the court will conclude that a parent cannot be found, it will require evidence of the efforts made to locate the parent. Establishing that a parent is incapable of consenting to the adoption will normally require medical evidence of incapacity. Where parental incapacity is of a temporary nature, it is unlikely that a court would dispense with the parent's consent immediately.

(b) *The parent or guardian is withholding agreement unreasonably.* This is the most contentious of the grounds for dispensing with parental consent. Since adoption severs the legal link between the child and the birth parent, it can be argued that it would always be reasonable for the parent to want to retain the link. However, the courts take the approach that parents want the best for their children. Thus, a reasonable parent would agree to adoption in certain circumstances and, if those circumstances are present in the instant case, then any parent who withholds agreement is doing so "unreasonably". It is not simply the reaction of the parent before the court which is being considered, his or her reaction is judged against that of a hypothetical "reasonable parent" (*A v. B and* C (1971) S.C. (H.L.) 129 *per* Lord Reid at p. 141; *D and D v. F* (1994) S.C.L.R. 417; *P v. Lothian Regional Council*, above, *per* Lord Justice-Clerk Ross at p.74).

(c) *The parent or guardian has persistently failed, without reasonable cause, to fulfil one of the following parental responsibilities in relation to the child:*

 (i) the responsibility to safeguard and promote the child's health, development and welfare; or

 (ii) if the child is not living with him, the responsibility to maintain personal relations and direct contact with the child on a regular basis.

 The parental failure to fulfil the particular responsibility must be "persistent", so an occasional lapse will not be enough. Parental explanation for failure to discharge their responsibilities may amount to a reasonable excuse. For example, parental ill-health might be thought to be a reasonable excuse for a failure to meet the standard of the reasonable parent, while callous disregard would not. In *Angus Council Social Work Department, Petitioner* (1998), Lord Penrose expressed the view that "the branches of section 2(c) are not mutually exclusive" and could occur in the same case.

(d) *The parent or guardian has seriously ill-treated the child, whose reintegration into the same household as the parent or guardian is, because of the serious ill-treatment or for other reasons, unlikely.* "Serious ill-treatment" is not defined in the Act but would include abuse, whether physical, emotional or sexual in nature, and neglect. Serious ill-treatment itself is not enough to warrant a finding that this ground is established; the child's reintegration into the family must also be unlikely. Once serious ill-treatment has been established, the court must consider the likelihood of the child's reintegration into the family and, where such reintegration is unlikely, the reason is not important. The problem over reintegration may be wholly unconnected with the ill-treatment, as, for example, where the parent has become ill.

THE ADOPTION PROCESS

The Scottish Adoption Service and adoption agencies

Adoption is a serious matter and one which requires rigorous scrutiny. For that reason, adoptions cannot be arranged privately and anyone, other than an adoption agency, who arranges an adoption is liable to prosecution, as is anyone who makes the placement or anyone who receives the child in such circumstances (s. 11(1) and (3)). There are two exceptions to this rule. First, where the adopter is a relative of the child, making the arrangements and placing the child need not be undertaken by an adoption agency (s. 11(1)). Secondly, a children's hearing may make it a condition of supervision that a child should live with people who are prospective adopters (Children (Scotland) Act 1995, s. 70(3)). These exceptions aside, adoption arrangements must be made by a local authority or an approved adoption society, these organisations being known, for this purpose, as "adoption agencies". Every local authority is obliged to establish and maintain a service designed to meet the needs of adopted children, their parents and guardians, and adopters or potential adopters (1978 Act, s. 1(1)). These services are known collectively as the Scottish Adoption Service (s. 1(4)). Any voluntary organisation may apply for approval from the Secretary of State to act as an adoption society and approval is subject to strict criteria (s. 3).

Freeing for adoption

A special procedure exists which allows the court to declare a child free for adoption. Before an application for an adoption order can be made, the child must live with the prospective adopters for a period of time. While the birth parents may have indicated that they agree to the child being adopted, it is always possible that they will change their minds before the adoption order is made and this leaves the whole adoption process in a precarious position. For this reason, s. 18 provides for "freeing orders". Broadly, the effect of a freeing order is to vest all parental responsibilities and rights in the adoption agency and obviate the need for the birth parents to have any further involvement in the adoption process.

Only a local authority may apply for such an order. At first instance each parent or guardian of the child must agree to the granting of the order. However, the court can dispense with parental consent in the same way as it can dispense with parental consent to adoption, but subject to two additional requirements. It must be satisfied that the child has already been placed for adoption, or that it is likely that the child will be so placed. If the child's parents are not married, it must be satisfied that the father does not have parental responsibilities or rights; does not intend to apply for them; or that, if he did, it is likely that his application would be unsuccessful. Where the child is 12 years old or older, his or her consent is required before a freeing order may be granted, and any views a younger child wishes to express must be taken into account by the court. Unless he or she has declared a preference to have no future involvement in the child's adoption, each parent is entitled to a progress report from the local authority one year after the freeing order has been granted (s. 19). The progress report should indicate whether or not the child has been adopted and, if not, whether the child has been placed for adoption. If the child has not been adopted or placed for adoption, the parent or guardian may apply for revocation of the freeing order (s. 20).

Placement
A child may be placed for adoption only after all the options available for the child's future have been explored (s. 6A). The selection of suitable adopters requires consideration being given to the child's racial, religious, cultural and linguistic profile (s. 6(1)(b)(ii)). Thought should be given to whether there is a need to place the child in the same home as siblings and whether there should be continued contact with birth parents. Private placement of children for adoption is prohibited unless the child and the adopters are related and most placements are now undertaken by an adoption agency (s. 11(1)). If the child has been placed for adoption privately, the applicant for adoption must give the local authority notice of the intention to adopt at least three months before date of order and the local authority must investigate the case and report to the court (s. 22).

Where the applicant or one of them is a parent, step-parent or relative of the child, or the child has been placed with the applicant by an adoption agency, the adoption order may not be made until the child is 19 weeks old and unless the child has had a home with the applicants for the preceding 13 weeks (s. 13(1)). In all other circumstances, no adoption order may be made until the child is 12 months old and unless the child has had a home with the applicants for the preceding 12 months (s. 13(2)).

Restrictions on removal of child pending adoption
Where a local authority has placed a child with a person with a view to adoption and the parents of the child have consented to the placement, it is an offence for any person to remove the child without the permission of the adoption agency or the court (s. 27). Where a person who has provided a home for a child for five years gives notice to the local authority of his or her intention to apply to adopt the child, it is an offence to remove the child from that person's care either

prior to the making of the application for an adoption order or for a period of three months after the receipt by the local authority of the notification of intention, whichever occurs first (s. 28). Where the child was in the care of the local authority prior to having a home with the applicant and remains in local authority care, the local authority can only remove the child in accordance with the procedure for return of a child placed for adoption or with the leave of a court (ss. 28(3), 30 and 31). In addition, the child's removal may be authorised by a children's hearing (s. 28(4)).

Application to court

The application for an adoption order is competent in either the Court of Session or the sheriff court, with most adoption orders being dealt with in the sheriff court, and the proceedings will be in private unless the court directs otherwise (ss. 56 and 57). A curator *ad litem* will be appointed to safeguard the child's interest and a reporting officer will be appointed to witness agreements to adoption (s. 58(1)). The court grants or refuses the adoption and may make it subject to such conditions as it thinks fit (s. 12(6)). In addition, the court may postpone the determination of the adoption application and make an order vesting parental responsibilities and rights in respect of the child in the applicants for a probationary period of up to two years (s. 25). Where the court refuses to grant the adoption order the child is returned to the adoption agency (s. 30(3)). All adoptions are registered in the Adopted Children's Register (s. 45).

THE EFFECTS OF ADOPTION

An adoption order vests all parental responsibilities and rights in relation to the child in the adopters (s. 12(1)) and, as a general rule, the child is no longer regarded as the child of his or her birth parents (s. 39). Where a child is adopted by a married couple, he or she is treated by the legal system as the "legitimate" child of the couple (s. 39(1)(a)). Where the adopter is a single person, the child is regarded as that person's "legitimate" child (s. 39(1)(b)). It will be remembered that, in the case of step-parent adoption, only the step-parent actually adopts the child and the birth parent to whom the step-parent is married retains his or her original status. The effect is that the child is treated as the child of that couple (s. 39(1)(c)). Where a child has been adopted by one of his or her parents and that person subsequently marries the other birth parent, the adoption does not prevent the child's subsequent legitimation (s. 39(2)). Thus, the general effect of adoption is to create a new family unit with all the attendant legal consequences. However, the following special effects and limitations on adoption should be noted:

(a) *The prohibited degrees for purposes of marriage.* The adoption order does not terminate the relationship between the child and birth relatives for the purpose of the prohibited degrees of marriage. In addition, marriage between an adopted child and an adoptive parent is prohibited. Two children adopted into the same family, but otherwise unrelated, may marry (1978 Act, s. 41(1) and the Marriage (Scotland) Act 1977, s. 2 and Sched. 1).

(b) *Incest.* Adoption has no effect for the purpose of the law of incest in so far as birth relatives are concerned, and sexual intercourse between the adoptive child and the adoptive parent is prohibited (1978 Act, s. 41(1) and Criminal Law (Consolidation) (Scotland) Act 1995, s. 1).

(c) *Pensions and certain insurance policies.* Adoption does not terminate any entitlement the child had to receive a pension (1978 Act, s. 42). Where the birth parent has taken out an insurance policy with a friendly society or certain other institutions, the policy is not terminated by adoption but is transferred to the adoptive parents who acquire the rights and liabilities under the policy (1978 Act, s. 43).

(d) *Succession.* The modern position is that the adopted child takes a full place in his or her adoptive family for succession purposes, subject to the remaining exception that adoption has no effect on succession to titles, honours and coats of arms. This does not apply where the adoption took place before September 10, 1964 and certain transitional provisions apply.

(e) *Nationality or immigration.* A child who is a citizen of the United Kingdom and colonies retains that status even if adopted by persons who are not (1978 Act, s. 41(2)). Where a foreign child is adopted by a United Kingdom citizen the child acquires United Kingdom nationality (British Nationality Act 1981, s. 1(5) and (6)).

(f) *Contact with the birth family.* The traditional view that adoption should terminate all contact between the child and the birth family has been challenged, not least because of the number of older children being adopted and the prevalence of step-parent adoptions. The term "open adoption" should be used with care, since it may mean many different practical arrangements in different circumstances. At a minimum, it may involve the exchange of information between the birth parents and the adopters in the early stage, with the exchange continuing, in some cases, but no direct contact between the birth parents and the child. However, it may involve direct contact between the child and his or her birth parents or other birth relatives and such an arrangement is known as "adoption with contact". When the court makes an adoption order it may attach "such terms and conditions as the court thinks fit" (s. 6(6)). After some initial doubt (*A v. B* (1987)), the courts accepted that this power could be used to provide for contact between a child and a birth parent or parents, where this will be of some benefit to the child (*B v. C* (1996)).

INTER-COUNTRY AND FOREIGN ADOPTION

As a result of the small number of children available for adoption in Scotland and of sympathy for the plight of children who are suffering deprivation in other parts of the world, inter-country adoption has gained popularity. Special rules apply to such adoptions and, as a party to the Hague Convention on Jurisdiction, Applicable Law and Recognition of Decrees Relating to Adoptions (1978), the United Kingdom has implemented special rules on adoptions involving the small number of other countries which have ratified it (1978 Act, s. 17). It is expected that the more recent Hague Convention on Adoption (1993), which utilises the mechanism of Central Authorities, already proven to be effective in the context of international child abduction, will attract greater support and will result in further domestic legislation. At present, the real control of foreign adoption is exercised through immigration law and the recognition of non-Convention adoptions. An adoption order made in England, Wales, Northern Ireland, the Isle of Man or the Channel Islands is an adoption order within the meaning of the 1978 Act and is recognised as such (s. 38(1)(c)). "Overseas adoptions" are recognised in Scotland and are regulated by the statutory instruments in force governing "adoptions of children appearing to [the Secretary of State] to be effected under the law of any country outside Great Britain" (ss. 38(1)(d) and 65(2)). Where an adoption does not fall within one of these categories, it may still be recognised at common law, and certainly the 1978 Act countenances recognition of other kinds of adoptions (s. 38(1)(e)).

Further reading
P. G. B. McNeill, *Adoption of Children in Scotland* (3rd ed., 1998, W. Green)
E. E. Sutherland, *Child and Family Law* (T & T Clark, 1999), chap. 8
A. B. Wilkinson and K. McK. Norrie, *The Law of Parent and Child in Scotland* (2nd ed., W. Green, 1999), chap. 4

---

5. PARENTAL RESPONSIBILITIES AND RIGHTS

Like other areas of law, the question of precisely what responsibilities parents owe to their children, and what rights they have in respect of them, developed over time. When the Scottish Law Commission turned its attention to these matters, it found that the law was in need of major reform (*Report on Family Law* (1992)). Part I of the Children (Scotland) Act 1995 is largely a product of its recommendations. References in this chapter are to the 1995 Act unless otherwise stated.

PARENTAL RESPONSIBILITIES

The 1995 Act provides a clear statement of what responsibilities parents have towards their children. Parental responsibilities exist only so far as is practicable and in the interests of the child (s. 1(1)). The child, or anyone acting on the child's behalf, has title to sue or defend in proceedings in respect of parental responsibilities (s. 1(3)). Parental responsibilities are:

(a)   *To safeguard and promote the child's health, development and welfare* (s. 1(1)(a)). This requires, not only that parents should protect the child's health, welfare and development, but that they should foster these interests actively. Clearly, a parent is required to meet the child's basic physical needs like housing, food and clothing. Providing for the child's welfare encompasses such matters as physical and psychological welfare and includes not only issues like safety, but also the provision of adequate medical care (*Finlayson (Applicant)* (1989); *McKechnie v. McKechnie* (1990)).

(b)   *To provide, in a manner appropriate to the stage of development of the child, (i) direction; and (ii) guidance* (s. 1(1)(b)). The line between direction, connoting instructions, and guidance, suggesting a more advisory role, will not always be clear cut. It should be remembered that the parental responsibility operates only where practicable and in the child's interests and alongside the child's rights to make decisions and the rights of third parties in certain contexts.

(c)   *If the child is not living with the parent, to maintain personal relations and direct contact with the child on a regular basis* (s. 1(1)(c)). The Act refers to "personal relations" as well as direct contact. This suggests communication on an emotional and psychological level, as well as simple presence. Essentially, a parent is required, at the very least, to keep in touch with a child, on a regular basis, where they are not living in the same household.

(d)   *To act as the child's legal representative* (s. 1(1)(d)). Essentially, there are three strands to this responsibility, but it is important to remember that children below the age of 16 have certain limited legal capacity of their own (Age of Legal Capacity (Scotland) Act 1991, discussed in chapter 3). First, the parental role involves administering any property belonging to the child (s. 15(5)(a)). Where the child's parents, as legal representatives, administer property on the child's behalf, their actions are governed by the detailed provisions in ss. 9 and 10 of the 1995 Act. The second strand to acting as the child's representative involves consenting to any transaction where the child is incapable of so acting on his or her own behalf (s. 15(5)(b)). The third is the parental role in litigation. Essentially, the duty of a legal representative is to sue and defend in civil proceedings on behalf of a person who cannot do that for himself or herself, or where the child does not wish to do so (s. 15(6)).

In order to avoid any doubt about the lingering effect of common law responsibilities which may have existed in the past and the interaction of the 1995 Act with other statutes, the Act itself makes it clear that its provisions supersede the prior common law but do not affect specific parental responsibilities set out in other statutes (s. 1(4)). So, for example, the obligations in respect of aliment and child support are unaltered by the 1995 Act, as are obligations in respect of education.

The responsibilities in respect of promoting health, development and welfare, providing direction, maintaining contact and legal representation all cease when the "child" reaches the age of 16 (s. 1(2)(a)). The responsibility to provide guidance lasts a little longer, until the "child" is 18 (s. 1(2)(b)).

PARENTAL RIGHTS

Parental rights exist in order that parents can fulfil their parental responsibilities (s. 2(1)) and they are subject to the same qualifications. Thus, they can only be exercised so far as is practicable and in the interests of the child. All of the parental rights terminate when the child reaches the age of 16 (s. 2(7)). As we shall see, parental rights mirror parental responsibilities. Parental rights are the rights:

(a) *To have the child living with him or her or otherwise to regulate the child's residence* (s. 2(1)(a)). The right to determine a child's residence becomes relevant between family members when a dispute arises, usually because the parents separate or have never lived together, although other family members may ask the court to regulate residence, as may the child.

(b) *To control, direct or guide, in a manner appropriate to the stage of development of the child, the child's upbringing* (s. 2(1)(b)). This is the corollary of the parental responsibility to provide direction and guidance to a child. However, it should be noted that the word "control" has been added, although it is doubtful that it adds anything to the content of the provision. It should be noted that, whereas the parental *responsibility* in respect of guidance lasts until the child is 18, the parental *right* to guide ends on the child's 16th birthday.

(c) *If the child is not living with the parent, to maintain personal relations and direct contact with the child on a regular basis* (s. 2(1)(c)). This parental right is the mirror image of the parental responsibility to maintain personal relations and direct contact. Essentially, the parent is being given the right to do that which he or she is obliged to do.

(d) *To act as the child's legal representative* (s. 2(1)(d)). Again, the parental right simply reflects the parental responsibility to act as the child's legal representative and is subject to the same qualifications.

The 1995 Act makes it clear that its provisions supersede the prior common law but do not affect specific parental responsibilities set out in other statutes (s. 2(5)). So, for example, parental rights in respect of a child's education remain.

WHO HAS PARENTAL RESPONSIBILITIES AND PARENTAL RIGHTS AUTOMATICALLY?

Parental responsibilities and parental rights are acquired *automatically* by:

(a) *The child's mother* (s. 3(1)(a)). All mothers acquire parental responsibilities and rights automatically from the moment of the child's birth.

(b) *The child's father, but only if he has been married to the mother at the time of the child's conception or subsequently* (s. 3(1)(b)). All "married fathers" are treated in the same way as are mothers, being endowed with automatic parental responsibilities and rights from the moment of the child's birth. In this context, "marriage" includes one which is voidable and one which is void but which both the parties believed in good faith to be valid at the time it was entered into (s. 3(2)). As we shall see, "unmarried fathers" (*i.e.* fathers who are not married to the child's mother) are treated differently.

No other persons acquire parental responsibilities or rights *automatically*. However, it must be remembered that this is no more than a starting point and the position may change subsequently. As we shall see, these parental responsibilities may be restricted or removed by a court (s. 11). A children's hearing may make a decision that has an enormous practical impact on the exercise of parental rights by, for example, requiring that the child should live somewhere other than with the parents (s. 70). Where the child is adopted subsequently, the original parental responsibilities and rights come to an end and the adopters acquire them afresh (Adoption (Scotland) Act 1978, s. 39). In addition, a host of persons may apply to the court for an order in relation to parental responsibilities and rights (s. 11) and how the courts approach this issue will be considered presently. First, we will consider the position of the unmarried father.

PARENTAL RESPONSIBILITIES AND RIGHTS AGREEMENTS

Unmarried fathers do not acquire parental responsibilities and rights automatically. It should be noted that the Scottish Law Commission recommended the removal of all distinctions linked to parental marital status (*Report on Family Law* (1992), Rec. 88), a position consistent with the U.N. Convention on the Rights of the Child (Arts 2 and 18). Parliament chose to reject that recommendation and, instead, made a small concession by providing for a special form of agreement that the child's mother can make with the father, giving him full parental responsibilities and rights (s. 4). Such agreements are only possible between the child's parents, irrespective of the age of the parents, and can only be made where the mother, herself, has full responsibilities and rights. The agreement must be in a form prescribed by the Secretary of State for Scotland and registered in the Books of Council and Session. Such agreements, once registered, are stated to be "irrevocable" (s. 4(4)) although, as is always the case with parental responsibilities and rights, the court retains its jurisdiction over the matter (s. 11).

APPLICATIONS TO THE COURT IN RESPECT OF PARENTAL RESPONSIBILITIES AND PARENTAL RIGHTS

Courts are not usually the best place to resolve disputes over the future arrangements for the care of children and the great increase in the use of mediation, in finding a workable solution, is to be welcomed. Inevitably, some cases do end up in court and the challenge for the legal system is to allow anyone with a legitimate concern about a child's future to bring the case before a court armed with adequate powers to deal with every situation.

Who may apply?
The following persons may make applications:

(a) *Any person who does not have and never has had parental responsibilities or parental rights in relation to the child but claims an interest* (s. 11(3)(i)). This is the broadest and most far-reaching category of potential applicants and covers anyone who has never had parental responsibilities or parental rights in relation to the child. The applicant must "claim an interest"; that is, show some legitimate concern or connection with the child (*F v. F* (1991)). While applications will often be made by unmarried fathers, step-parents or relatives, non-relatives may use this provision.

(b) *Any person who has parental responsibilities or rights* (s. 11(3)(ii)). Where a person already has parental responsibilities and rights, he or she may apply to the court for regulation of them. Usually, the applicant is seeking to have someone else's parental responsibilities and rights regulated. Where, for example, married parents are divorcing, they will each have full parental responsibilities and rights. They need do nothing and each of them can continue with the same legal recognition of his or her status as a parent and agree the practical arrangements. If they cannot agree, either of them can go to the court and each will be seeking to remove or restrict the other's responsibilities and rights.

(c) *Any person who has had parental responsibilities or rights in relation to the child, but no longer has them and is not excluded by the Act* (s. 11(3)(iii)). Various people may have had parental responsibilities or rights in the past but have lost them. Some of them, like a parent who has lost them on the application of the other parent, can still go back to the court in the future in an attempt to re-establish some aspect of their role as parent. However, an application for an order under s. 11 may not be made by any person who had any parental responsibility or parental right but no longer has them because they have been: extinguished by an adoption order; transferred to an adoption agency by an order freeing the child for adoption; extinguished by an order under the Human Fertilisation and Embryology Act 1990 (s. 30(9)); or transferred to a local authority by a parental responsibilities order (s. 11(3)(iii) and (4)). The local authority has extensive powers in respect of children under Part II of the 1995 Act. For that reason, it is not permitted to use the provisions of s. 11 (s. 11(5)).

(d) *The child* (s. 11(5)). In the past, there was some doubt about whether or not a child could competently apply to the court for an order regulating parental rights being exercised over him or her. The 1995 Act puts the matter beyond doubt.

Action the court can take on its own initiative

Normally, the court will consider making an order because someone has made an application. However, the court can take the initiative in making an order. First, where no application has been made, or where the order sought by an applicant has been refused, the court can make a section 11 order nonetheless (s. 11(3)(b)). Secondly, if it appears to the court that any of the grounds for referring a child to a children's hearing (see chapter 7) is satisfied in relation to a child, it may refer the matter to the principal reporter, who will consider whether it is necessary to refer the child to a hearing (s. 54).

What can be applied for?

The 1995 Act provides that the court may make an order *in relation* to parental responsibilities, parental rights, guardianship or the administration of a child's property (s. 11(1)). Often, the pursuer will be applying to be given parental responsibilities or rights, but he or she may be seeking to have another person's rights removed or regulated. The court has very broad powers in granting any order it thinks fit (s. 11(2)). While section 11(2) places no limit on the orders the court may make, those most commonly applied for are residence orders and contact orders. Occasionally, a specific issue order may be sought to resolve a dispute over a particular matter such as whether the child can be taken abroad on holiday.

Court proceedings
Applications in relation to parental responsibilities and rights may be made alone or ancillary to another action in either the sheriff court or the Court of Session (s. 11(1)). The onus of proof in applications in respect of parental responsibilities and rights lies on the applicant (*Sanderson v. McManus* (1997)). The standard of proof is on the balance of probabilities (*F v. F* (1991)). The usual rules of evidence apply and, while hearsay evidence is admissible (Civil Evidence (Scotland) Act 1988, s. 2), it must be established that the child from whom the hearsay evidence is derived would be a competent witness (*Rees v. Lowe* (1990); *L v. L* (1996); *Sanderson v. McManus* (1997)).

Criteria for the court's decision
In reaching its decision, the court will apply the overarching principles:

(a) *The welfare of the child is the paramount consideration* (s. 11(7)(a)). Each case will depend on its own facts and circumstances, but courts in the past have considered such matters as physical welfare (*Clayton v. Clayton* (1995)), who will be looking after the child (*Brixey v. Lynas* (1994)), role models (*Casey v. Casey* (1989)), emotional welfare (*Geddes v. Geddes* (1987); *Early v. Early* (1989)), the impact of religion (*McKechnie v. McKechnie* (1990)), educational welfare (*Clayton v. Clayton* (1995)), and parental lifestyle (*Brixey v. Lynas* (1994)). Much has been written on what will serve or detract from a child's welfare and reference should be made to the further reading on this point.

(b) *The child must be given the opportunity to express his or her views and account will be taken of these views in the light of the child's age and maturity* (s. 11(7)(b)). Sometimes the child's views will be given very considerable weight (*Mason v. Mason* (1987)), but the child's age and maturity will be kept in mind (*Casey v. Casey* (1989)).

(c) *The court will not make any order unless to do so will be better than making no order at all* (s. 11(7)(a)).

FULFILLING PARENTAL RESPONSIBILITIES AND EXERCISING PARENTAL RIGHTS

Where more than one person has responsibilities and rights in respect of a child, the general rule is that each of the persons may exercise the right alone, without the consent of the other (s. 2(2)). However, the freedom to exercise parental rights alone does not entitle a person to remove a child from the United Kingdom without appropriate consent (s. 2(3)). The overarching principles apply to fulfilling parental responsibilities and exercise of parental rights and the Act makes special provision, requiring any person who is taking a *major decision* in this context to give the child the opportunity to express his or her views and to take these views into account in the light of the child's age and maturity (s. 6). While a person who has responsibilities or rights may not surrender or transfer any part of these, the holder is permitted to arrange for these to be exercised or met by another person acting on the holder's behalf (s. 3(5)). No arrangement of this sort affects a person's liability for failure to meet parental responsibilities (s. 3(6)). This power to delegate covers a very wide range of possible situations and would include a parent who uses an occasional babysitter, a full-time nanny, or day care.

CHILD ABDUCTION

As we have seen, the legal system provides extensive machinery to regulate where a child may live and with whom. Despite that, a parent may be dissatisfied with the arrangements and may take the law into his or her own hands, either by taking the child away, in breach of an agreement or a court order, or by refusing to return the child after an authorised visit. Illegal removal of a child from a person entitled to control the child's residence is governed by both civil and criminal law, as is wrongful retention of the child. Within the United Kingdom, special provisions ensure the quick return of children taken from one jurisdiction to another (Family Law Act 1996). The common law offence of *plagium* is the offence of stealing a child from his or her parents and the offence can be committed by a parent who has no right to determine the child's residence (*Downie v. H.M. Advocate* (1984)).

Since child abduction may also involve taking a child out of the United Kingdom, it is important to be aware of the Hague Convention on the Civil Aspects of International Child Abduction (1980) and the European Convention on Recognition and Enforcement of Decisions concerning Custody of Children and on the Restoration of Custody of Children (1980), since the United Kingdom has ratified both and implemented them through the Child Abduction and Custody Act 1985. The Hague Convention on Jurisdiction, Applicable Law, Recognition, Enforcement and Co-operation in respect of Parental Responsibility and Measures for the Protection of Children (1996) will also be important in the future. Broadly, the Conventions create mutual obligations between contracting states to effect the speedy return of children to the appropriate country. Where a child has been abducted from Scotland to a Convention country, then the parent in Scotland can make use of the provisions. Conversely, the law provides for a child who has been brought to Scotland illegally being returned to his or her place of habitual residence.

Where a child has been abducted to a country which is not a party to the Conventions, the party seeking to secure the child's return will have to rely on the domestic law of that country and, sometimes, the prospects of the child's return are not good. It is an offence for a "person connected with a child" to remove the child from Scotland without the consent of the child's parents, guardians and any person named by a court as the person with whom the child should live (Child Abduction Act 1984).

FINANCIAL SUPPORT FOR CHILDREN

Scots law has always recognised that parents are obliged to support their children. Only when they are unable to do so, does the obligation fall on the state. The traditional mechanism, the law on aliment, which is administered by the courts, is now found in the Family Law (Scotland) Act 1985. In 1991, a separate system for dealing with financial support for most children was introduced by the Child Support Act 1991 which created a complicated, formula-driven, administrative procedure, under which responsibility for the assessment and collection of financial support for children was to be passed over to the Child Support Agency (CSA). From 2001, the current, rather complicated, child support formulae will be replaced by liability based on a simple percentage of net income. Both aliment and child support apply in particular cases and it is necessary to look at each.

Child support

Child support applies only where the following parties are present:

(a) a "qualifying child". Broadly, this means a child under the age of 16, but unmarried children can be covered up to the age of 18, if the parent is still claiming state benefit in respect of them, or 19 if the child is still at school (s. 55). For there to be a "qualifying child", one or both of the parents must be an "absent parent" (s. 3(1)).

(b) an "absent parent". This particularly insensitive term will be replaced by the more objective term "non-resident parent". Such a parent is one who is not living in the same household as the child, where the child has a home with a person with care (s. 3(2)). "Parent" covers only mothers and fathers and does not include step-parents (s. 54).

(c) a "person with care". This is the person with whom the child has a home or who usually provides the day-to-day care for the child (s. 3(3)) and will often be one of the child's parents (known as the "parent with care").

Essentially, the child support system applies to two categories of people, those who must use it and those who choose to do so. Where a parent with care is in receipt of a broad range of state benefits, including income support and family credit, he or she must authorise the Secretary of State to take action to recover child support maintenance from the absent parent (s. 6(1)). Where a person is required to give such authorisation, he or she is obliged to co-operate in seeking a maintenance assessment and in providing the necessary information and, in particular, information enabling the absent parent to be traced (s. 6(5)–(9)). The Act provides that, where there are reasonable grounds for believing that co-operation in seeking a maintenance assessment would expose the mother, or any child living with her, to the risk of "harm or undue distress", then she will not be required to give authorisation (s. 6(2) and (3)). Where a parent with care fails to co-operate as required by the Act and does not fall within the exemption, that parent's benefits may be cut by up to 40 per cent for up to three years, with possible extensions of this period for as long as she refuses to disclose the father's identity (s. 46).

In addition to those who must use the child support system, it is available to many others. Anyone who qualifies as a person with care, whether a parent or not, may apply for a maintenance assessment under the Act, as can the absent parent (s. 4(1)). Consistent with the general principles recognising the empowerment of children aged 12 or over, any such child who is habitually resident in Scotland can apply for a maintenance assessment (s. 7(1)). Applications for a maintenance assessment cannot be made where there is already an assessment in force (s. 4(9)).

How the system works
The assessment of maintenance due by the absent parent is calculated according to a number of inter-related formulae set out in the 1991 Act and the regulations. The key elements of the calculation are: the maintenance requirement; assessable income; the rate of deduction; and the protected income level. In its original form, the Act allowed for no deviation from its rigid formulation but, as a result of injustices and criticisms, a system of "departures", allowing a modest amount of discretion, was introduced by the Child Support Act 1995. Given that the system will be altered radically from 2001, there is no need to go into the details of how child support is calculated.

Decisions on child support can be challenged through reviews and appeals. The original decision of the child support officer can be reviewed internally at the request of a person with care, an absent parent or the child (s. 18). Thereafter, appeal lies to the Child Support Appeal Tribunal (s. 20) and "on a question of law" to a Child Support Commissioner (s. 24). Further appeal lies to the courts on questions of law (s. 25).In addition to review as the first stage in the appeal process, the Act provides for regular periodic review and review at the request of interested parties, in certain circumstances (ss. 16–18).

Co-operation with the CSA is enforced through the threat of a reduction in benefits. Once a maintenance assessment has been made, the CSA has a broad range of powers to enable it to recover unpaid child support. It can have sums deducted from a person's wages and obtain and enforce a court order (ss. 31–33). Ultimately, imprisonment is the sanction for failure to pay child support (s. 40).

Child support and the courts
The main thrust of the 1991 Act is to exclude the courts from determining issues of financial support for children. Where a child support officer "would have jurisdiction to make a maintenance assessment . . . no court shall exercise any power which it would otherwise have to make, vary or revive any maintenance order" (s. 8). There are a host of exceptions to this general rule. Many of them are set out explicitly in the 1991 Act, others implicit in it. The most important arise in respect of "top up" awards, where a parent is particularly wealthy (s. 8(6)); additional payments to cover educational expenses, like school fees (s. 8(7)); and expenses attributable to a child's disability (s. 8(8) and (9)). In addition, child support is inapplicable where one of the parties is habitually resident abroad (s. 44).

Aliment

Aliment remains relevant where the child support legislation does not apply and is of particular significance where the obligation to support a child falls on a non-parent, like a step-parent or other relative. Aliment may be claimed by a person up to the age of 25, who is still in full-time education or training, and is of particular importance to students. The Family Law (Scotland) Act 1985 is the relevant statute here.

For the purpose of aliment, a "child" is a person:

(a)   under 18 years old, or,
(b)   under 25 years old, "who is reasonably and appropriately undergoing instruction at an educational establishment, or training for employment or for a trade, profession or vocation" (s. 1(5)).

Such a child is owed an obligation of aliment by:

(a)   his or her mother (s. 1(1)(a));
(b)   his or her father (s. 1(1)(b));
(c)   any person who has "accepted" the child into his or her family (s. 1(1)(c)). "Acceptance" denotes more than simply living under the same roof as the child, and can render other family members, like an aunt or uncle (*Inglis v. Inglis* (1987)) or a step-parent, liable for aliment. A person is not regarded as accepting a child where the child has been boarded out to that person by a local or public authority or a voluntary organisation;
(d)   the executor of a deceased person or any person who has been enriched by succession to the estate of a deceased person owing the obligation (s. 1(4)).

Where more than one person owes an obligation to aliment, there is no automatic order of liability, although when aliment is being sought from one person, the obligations of other persons will be taken into account (s. 4(2)).

How much?

The obligation of aliment is to provide "such support as is reasonable in the circumstances" (s. 1(2)), having regard to:

(a) the needs and resources of parties (s. 4(1)(a)). The present and foreseeable needs and resources of both the pursuer and defender are relevant here. For example, where a schoolgirl had a part-time job, her father was able to argue that the amount of aliment payable by him should be reduced (*Wilson v. Wilson* (1987)). In assessing the parties' respective needs and resources, the court will look at actual income, expenditure in respect of appropriate items, and at evidence of an individual's lifestyle including such matters as foreign holidays (*Joshi v. Joshi* (1998)).

(b) the earning capacities of parties (s. 4(1)(b)). It should be noted that it is not simply the actual earnings of the parties which are relevant, but their earning *capacities*. Where a person has a well-paid job and gives it up when confronted with a claim for aliment, what he or she was earning will usually be taken into account, as a reflection of earning capacity.

(c) all the circumstances of the case (s. 4(1)(c)). This consideration acknowledges that every case will turn on its own facts. However, amongst other relevant circumstances mentioned in the Act is the fact that the defender is supporting another person, whether or not he or she is under an obligation to do so (s. 4(3)(a)).

A person's conduct is irrelevant unless it would be "manifestly inequitable" to ignore it (s. 4(3)(b)).

Defences

The fact that a child is living with the defender is no bar to raising an action for aliment (s. 2(6)). However, it is open to the defender to demonstrate that he or she is fulfilling the alimentary obligation by supporting the child in his or her own home and that he or she will continue to do so (s. 2(7)). In addition, where the child is over the age of 16, it is open to the defender to make an offer to maintain the child in his or her own household. However, such an offer only constitutes a good defence where it would be reasonable to expect the child to accept the offer (s. 2(8)). In assessing "reasonableness", the court is directed to have regard to "any conduct, decree or other circumstances" (s. 2(9)). An offer of this kind is no defence where the child is below the age of 16 (s. 2(8)).

How does aliment work?

An action for aliment may be raised in either the Court of Session or sheriff court (s. 2(1)), and may be brought by way of an independent action or in the course of other proceedings (s. 2(2)). The action may be raised by the child or, on behalf of a child under 18, by a parent, a guardian, or a person with whom the child lives or who is seeking a residence order (s. 2(3)). A woman may raise an action on behalf of her unborn child, but the action will not be heard and disposed of until after the birth (s. 2(5)).

The court may grant decree in an action for aliment and, in so doing, may make two kinds of awards. The first, and most common, is to order the making of periodical payments for a definite or indefinite period or until a specific event happens (s. 3(1)(a)). Secondly, it may also order the making of an alimentary payment of an occasional or special nature to cover expenses like a school trip (s. 3(1)(b)). Such awards should not be used as a means of substituting a lump sum for periodical payments (s. 3(2)). In granting decree, the court can backdate an award (s. 3(1)(c)) and a smaller sum than that sought may be awarded (s. 3(1)(d)).

Either the pursuer or the defender may request variation or recall of an order for aliment on showing that there has been a material change of circumstances (s. 5(1)). What is, or is not, a material change of circumstances will turn on the individual facts of each case and the only such circumstance spelt out in the Act is the making of a child maintenance assessment under the Child Support Act 1991 (s. 5(1A)). The court has the power to backdate any variation (s. 5(2)) and order repayment of sums paid under the original decree. In the course of considering variation or recall, it may make an interim award (s. 5(3)).

Further reading
E. E. Sutherland, *Child and Family Law* (T & T Clark, 1999), chaps 5 and 6
A. B. Wilkinson and K. McK. Norrie, *The Law of Parent and Child in Scotland* (2nd ed., W. Green, 1999), chaps 8–14.

---

6. CHILD PROTECTION

The legal system takes a number of different approaches to child protection. It defines who has responsibilities for children, what they are, and adjudicates in cases of dispute (see chapter 5). It seeks to deny children access to particular commodities or dangers (see chapter 3). In this chapter we will consider the role of the state through the duties placed on local authorities and court orders designed to protect children.

Reform of aspects of the child protection system was already being proposed when the *Orkney Case* (*Sloan v. B* (1991)) hit the headlines. There, nine children from four separate families were removed from their homes by social workers acting on the authority of emergency court orders amid allegations that the children had been victims of organised sexual abuse. The children were separated from their families and each other for 37 days before being returned home without the allegations having been fully addressed in court. Such was the concern about the handling of the case that a public inquiry was set up and, as a result of its recommendations (*Report into the Inquiry into the Removal of Children from Orkney in 1991* (1992)), changes were made to the legislation and supporting guidelines. The Children (Scotland) Act 1995, Pt II, now governs child protection and references below are to that Act unless otherwise stated. More recently, concern has focused on children in institutional care and, while this has sometimes centred on abuse which took place many years ago (*Edinburgh's Children* (1999)), recommendations for reform of the current system have been made (*Children's Safeguards Review* (1997)).

LOCAL AUTHORITY OBLIGATIONS TO CHILDREN

The starting point is that children should normally be cared for within their own families (s. 22(1)(b)) and it is only where the child's welfare cannot be served adequately in that setting that removal becomes an option. While the 1995 Act places much of the responsibility for child protection on the local authority, which it fulfils largely through its social work department, it should be remembered that others, like educators, health care professionals, the police, the Royal Scottish Society for the Prevention of Cruelty to Children and voluntary organisations, all play crucial roles. That the local authority should approach its obligations to children in a co-ordinated manner is demonstrated by the fact that it is required to prepare, publish, and keep under review a plan of the provision of services to children in its area (s. 19).

The local authority often has particular duties towards "children in need". This is a term with a special statutory meaning and a "child in need" is one:

(a) who is unlikely to achieve or maintain a reasonable standard of health or development unless services are provided for him or her by the local authority; or

(b) whose health or development is likely to be impaired significantly unless such services are provided; or

(c) who is disabled; or who is affected adversely by the disability of another member of his or her family (s. 93(4)(a)).

The local authority is *obliged* to safeguard and promote their welfare by providing services for the child directly and providing services for another member of the child's family or for the family as a whole, if such provision is designed to safeguard or promote the child's welfare (s. 22(1)(a)).

Day care for pre-school and other children

In respect of children in need, each local authority *must* provide day care for children under five years old (s. 27(1)) and after school care

(s. 27(3)). While it *may* provide such care for other children, it is not obliged to do so. In addition, the local authority oversees the provision of private day care for children under the age of eight, where it is provided through day care or child minding, through a system of registration (Children Act 1989, Pt X).

Children with disabilities and those affected by the disability of another person

A child may have a disability and require special assistance or facilities, or may be affected by the disability of another family member, like a parent or a sibling. Such children fall within the definition of children in need. The local authority *must* provide assistance to such children in order to "to minimise the adverse effect" of the disability on them and to give them "the opportunity to lead lives which are as normal as possible" (s. 23(1)).

Provision of accommodation for children

The local authority is *obliged* to provide accommodation for a child below the age of 18 where he or she appears to require it because: no one has parental responsibilities for the child; the child is lost or abandoned; or the child's carer is prevented, whether or not permanently and for whatever reason, from providing suitable accommodation or care (s. 25(1)). In addition, the local authority *may* provide a child with accommodation if it considers that to do so would safeguard or promote the child's welfare (s. 25(2)). Accommodation *may* be provided for 18- to 21-year-olds in similar circumstances (s. 25(3)).

One way in which the local authority may discharge its obligation to look after children is through the use of foster care. Organisation of foster care is the responsibility of the local authority and the Fostering of Children (Scotland) Regulations 1996 provide detailed regulation of the operation of fostering. It should be remembered that a child living with foster carers is still being "looked after" by the local authority and its obligations to the child continue.

Obligations to children being looked after by the local authority

The local authority *must* safeguard and promote the welfare of every child it is looking after and the child's welfare must be its paramount concern (s. 17(1)(a)). It must provide advice and assistance to prepare the child for a time when the local authority is no longer looking after him or her (s. 17(2)). In so far as it is consistent with the child's welfare, the local authority must promote personal relations and direct contact on a regular basis between the child and any person with parental responsibilities in relation to the child (s. 17(1)(c)). Where a local authority is looking after a child, it must take reasonable steps to ascertain the child's views before making *any decision* with respect to the child and take those views into account in the light of the child's age and maturity (ss. 17(3)(a) and 17(4)(a)). In addition, the local authority is obliged to ascertain the views of the child's parents, non-parents who have parental rights in respect of the child, and any other person the local authority considers relevant, and to take any views expressed by these persons into account (ss. 17(3)(b)–(d) and 17(4)(b)). In fulfilling its obligations to the child, the local authority is permitted to act in a manner inconsistent with its duties under s. 17 where such action is necessary to protect members of the public from serious harm (s. 17(5)).

After-care for young people leaving care
Where a young person was being looked after by the local authority at the time he or she ceased to be of school age or at any time thereafter, the local authority is *obliged* to advise, guide and assist that young person until he or she reaches 19, unless the local authority is satisfied that the young person's welfare does not require it (s. 29(1)). In addition, the young person may request such advice, guidance and assistance until he or she is 21 and the local authority *may* provide it (s. 29(2)).

Financial assistance towards expenses of education or training
Where a young person has been looked after by the local authority at the time he or she ceased to be of school age or at any time thereafter, the local authority *may* make a grant to the young person to meet expenses connected with education or training or contribute towards accommodation or maintenance of such a young person while he or she is under 21 (s. 30(1) and (2)). Where a local authority has provided this form of assistance prior to the young person reaching the age of 21, it *may* continue to provide it thereafter (s. 30(3)).

COURT ORDERS

Often the local authority can provide families with support and thus enable a child to remain at home. However, it may be that the local authority is concerned that, despite its assistance, a child is at risk in the home environment. In other cases, the local authority may be convinced that a child is at risk in the family home. It must then consider which, if any, of the orders described below it should seek.

Overarching principles
The overarching principles, or child lawyer's mantra, which we have seen operating in the family setting also apply in the context of child protection. When a court or a children's hearing is reaching a decision it must usually consider these principles. However, they do not apply to all such decisions and may be subject to qualification.

(a) *The welfare of that child throughout his or her childhood shall be the paramount consideration* (s. 16(1)). The welfare principle applies throughout Part II of the 1995 Act, and it is welfare throughout the child's childhood, that is, until the child reaches the age of 18, that is relevant. Deviation from this principle is permitted, for example, "for the purpose of protecting members of the public from serious harm" (s. 16(5)).

(b) *The child must be given the opportunity to express his or her views in certain circumstances and regard must be had to these views* (s. 16(2) and (4)). As we shall see in chapter 7, the child's participation has always been central to the children's hearings system. In the context of courts, children must usually be given the opportunity to participate when decisions are being taken about them. However, while the child's views are relevant to most decisions under this part of the Act, they need not be considered in all cases. For example, a sheriff need not consider them when deciding whether to grant a child protection order.

(c) *An order should be made unless making the order would be better than making no order at all* (s. 16(3)). Presumed non-intervention applies to most decisions under Part II of the Act where a child's views are relevant. Where presumed non-intervention applies, it determines whether an order should or should not be granted. Once an order has been granted, the appropriate level of intervention is not subject to any presumption of non-intervention.

Relevant persons

Before we look at the orders a court can make, it is important to be clear about what is meant by "relevant persons". This term was coined by the 1995 Act to indicate that people other than parents might be important in a child's life and to make those people part of the decision making process. Relevant persons are:

(a) any parent who has parental rights or responsibilities;
(b) any person in whom parental responsibilities or rights are vested by virtue of the Act; and
(c) any person who has or appears to have charge of or control over a child, otherwise than in the course of employment (s. 93(2)(iii) (c)).

Child Assessment Orders (CAOs)

A child assessment order provides for the opportunity to determine whether the local authority's suspicion of abuse or neglect is justified, where such assessment would not be possible without the court giving its authority, and may involve removing the child from the home (s. 55). Only a local authority may apply for a CAO and, before exercising his or her discretion to grant an order, the sheriff must be satisfied that:

(a) the local authority has reasonable grounds to suspect that the child is being so treated (or neglected) that he or she is suffering, or is likely to suffer, *significant harm*; and
(b) such assessment is necessary to establish whether the child is being so treated (or neglected); and

(c) such assessment is unlikely to be carried out, or be carried out satisfactorily, unless the order is granted (s. 55).

A CAO may be appropriate, for example, to authorise medical examination of the child in the face of parental opposition. It should be noted that the 1995 Act specifically preserves the child's right to consent to medical examination (s. 90). Thus, a CAO cannot be used to override the opposition of a child who understands what is involved. A CAO cannot last for more than seven days and it must specify when assessment is to begin (s. 55(3)). It may deal with other matters like where the child is to reside during assessment and who may have contact with the child (s. 55 (4) and (5)). Where a CAO results in the child's removal from home, he or she becomes a child being looked after by the local authority and the local authority acquires the responsibility for safeguarding his or her welfare (s. 17(1) and (6)(c)). Where an application is made for a CAO and the sheriff finds that the more stringent grounds justifying the granting of a child protection order are satisfied, the Act provides that he or she "shall" make the latter (s. 55(2)).

Having assessed the child, the local authority may conclude that its suspicions were unfounded and that no further action is required, or that there is some cause for concern, but that voluntary arrangements can be made with the family to address the concern. However, the local authority may conclude that the case should be referred to the Principal Reporter (see chapter 7) or that it should apply for an exclusion order or a child protection order.

Exclusion Orders (EOs)

The 1995 Act introduced a new kind of exclusion order, modelled on the kind available under the Matrimonial Homes (Family Protection) (Scotland) Act 1981 (see chapter 9), to provide for the removal of the alleged abuser from the family home (ss. 76–80). Previously, where there was concern over a child's safety, it was usually the child who was removed and it was likely that at least some children saw their removal as implying that the problem was somehow their fault. Only a local authority may apply for an EO and a sheriff may exclude a named person from a child's family home if he or she is satisfied that:

(a) the child has suffered, is suffering, or is likely to suffer, significant harm as a result of any conduct, or threatened or reasonably apprehended conduct, of the named person; and

(b) the making of the order (i) is necessary to protect the child, irrespective of whether the child is residing in the family home at the moment, and (ii) would better safeguard the child's welfare than removal of the child from the family home; and

(c) if the order is made there will be someone specified in the application (an "appropriate person") who is capable of looking after the child and any other family member who lives in the household and requires care and who is, or will be, residing in the family home (s. 76(2)).

However, an EO must be refused if to grant it would be "unjustifiable or unreasonable" (s. 76(9)–(11)). In assessing this criterion, the sheriff must consider all the circumstances of the case, including:

(a) the conduct of the members of the child's family;
(b) the respective needs and financial resources of the members of that family;
(c) the extent to which the home is used in connection with a trade, business or profession; and
(d) any requirement that the named person should reside in the family home, like the fact that it is let or occupied by an employee as an incident of employment.

He or she must then weigh these considerations in the light of the overarching principles (s. 16).

The named person and certain other people, like a landlord, have a right to be heard or represented before a final decision on the application for an EO is made (s. 76(3)). In the meantime, the sheriff may grant an interim EO (s. 76(4) and (6)). Where an EO is sought and the sheriff is satisfied that the conditions justifying a child protection order are satisfied, he or she may grant a child protection order (s. 76(8)). The effect of an EO is to suspend the named person's right of occupancy in the home to which the order relates and prevent him or her from entering that home except with the permission of the local authority which applied for the order (s. 77(1)). Various ancillary orders may be attached to an EO, like an interdict prohibiting the named person from removing relevant items from the home or prohibiting the named person from entering or remaining in a specified area within the vicinity of the home (s. 77(3)). At any time when an EO is in force, the local authority may apply to the sheriff for a power of arrest to be attached to it (s. 78). An EO under the 1995 Act lasts for no longer than six months and may last for a shorter period of time where that is specified in the order itself (s. 79(1) and (2)).

Child Protection Orders (CPOs)
CPOs were introduced by the 1995 Act to replace the older mechanism, the place of safety order, which had been the subject of so much criticism. CPOs are intended to be more flexible and there are detailed provisions on their implementation, review, duration, recall and variation. Application for a CPO may be made to a sheriff in *two distinct sets of circumstances* and the granting of a CPO is discretionary.

First, *any person* (including the child or a relative) may apply for a CPO on the basis that:

(a) the child is being so treated (or neglected) that he or she is suffering significant harm or that he or she will suffer such harm if not removed and kept in a place of safety or if he or she does not remain in the place where he or she is being accommodated; and

(b) the order is necessary to protect the child from such harm (or further harm) (s. 57(1)).

Secondly, *a local authority* may apply for a CPO on the basis that:

(a) the child is being so treated (or neglected) that he or she is suffering, or will suffer, significant harm, and

(b) it is making enquiries to allow it to decide whether it should take any action to safeguard the welfare of the child, and

(c) its enquiries are being frustrated by access to the child being unreasonably denied, such access being required as a matter of urgency (s. 57(2)).

In reaching his or her decision, the sheriff must regard the child's welfare as the paramount consideration (s. 16(1)). There is no requirement to take the child's views into account, although how the child feels about the possibility of being removed from home or detained elsewhere will be relevant in considering whether the order will serve the child's welfare. In addition, the local authority should have tried to ascertain the child's views (s. 17(3)). The sheriff must make an immediate decision on an application for a CPO (Act of Sederunt (Child Care and Maintenance Rules) 1997, r. 3.31). There is no appeal against the sheriff's decision to grant or refuse a CPO (s. 51(15)). In addition to authorising the removal and retention of a child, a CPO can provide that a child should not be removed from a specified place, require a person to produce the child, and provide that the location of the child's whereabouts should not be disclosed to particular persons (s. 57(4)). Similarly, the sheriff may make a direction on contact between the child and any other persons, like the child's parents (s. 58(1)).

Once granted, a CPO ceases to have effect if no attempt to implement it has been made within 24 hours (s. 60(1)). Where a CPO has resulted in a child being taken to a place of safety or kept in such a place, it must be subject to review on the second working day after implementation (s. 60(2)). Review may be by means of an application to the sheriff (s. 60) or a children's hearing (s. 59). In the latter case, there is the possibility of a second review, within two working days of the first children's hearings review, through an application to a sheriff (s. 60(7)). No CPO can remain in force beyond the eighth working day after implementation (ss. 60(6) and 65(2)). Usually a children's hearing will be arranged for that day. At that hearing, if it is believed that the child should remain in a place of safety, the hearing may grant a warrant authorising this (ss. 66(1) and 69(7)). At a later hearing what should happen to the child in the longer term will be considered and children's hearings are discussed in chapter 7.

Emergency protection where a CPO is not available

It is possible, particularly in rural areas, that no sheriff is on hand to consider an application for a CPO. For this reason, two short-term measures provide for emergency protection of children. First, a justice of the peace may consider an application for a CPO where it is not practicable for the application to be made to a sheriff (s. 61(1)–(4)). A CPO granted by a justice of the peace has much the same effect as a CPO granted by a sheriff. Secondly, a police officer may, without authorisation from a sheriff, take a child to a place of safety where the police officer has reasonable cause to believe that the conditions for making a CPO are satisfied, that it is not practicable to make an application to a sheriff, and that it is necessary in order to protect a child from significant harm (s. 61(5)). In each case, a child may not be kept at a place of safety for longer than 24 hours and it is envisaged that a CPO will be applied for, if necessary, within that time.

Parental Responsibilities Order (PRO)

There may be circumstances in which the local authority believes that it would be best for a child if it took over parental responsibilities and parental rights in respect of the child and the 1995 Act enables the local authority to apply for a PRO in order to do this (s. 86). Before the sheriff may grant a PRO, he or she must be satisfied, in respect of each relevant person, that he or she:

(a)   freely, and with full understanding of what is involved, agrees unconditionally that the order be made; or

(b)   is not known, cannot be found, or is incapable of giving consent; or

(c)   is withholding consent unreasonably; or

(d)   has persistently failed without reasonable cause to fulfill the parental responsibility to safeguard and promote the child's health, development and welfare or, if the child is not living with him or her, has failed to maintain personal relations and direct contact on a regular basis; or

(e)   has seriously ill-treated the child and the child's reintegration into the household is unlikely (s. 86(2)).

It will be noted that these conditions are similar to those required for dispensing with parental agreement to adoption which were discussed in chapter 4. In addition to one of the above conditions being satisfied, the sheriff must also be satisfied that to grant the PRO would be consistent with the child's welfare (s. 16(1)).

The effect of a PRO is to transfer "the appropriate parental rights and responsibilities", defined as all parental responsibilities and rights except the right to consent to an order freeing a child for adoption or an adoption order (s. 86(3)). In granting a PRO, the sheriff may make it subject to conditions as he or she considers appropriate (s. 86(5)). In addition, the 1995 Act makes detailed provision on the contact a child may have with certain persons and provides that the local authority shall allow reasonable contact between the child and any person who was either a responsible person prior to the granting of the PRO, or any person in whose favour a residence order or contact order was in force prior to the PRO being granted (s. 88(2)). In addition, the child, the local authority or any person with an interest may apply for a contact order (s. 88(3)) and the sheriff may make a contact order without any such an application being made (s. 88(4)). Any of these persons may apply for variation or discharge of a contact order (s. 88(5)) and the order ceases to have effect if the PRO itself terminates (s. 88(6)).

A PRO may be varied or discharged by the sheriff on the application of the local authority, the child, a person who was a relevant person prior to the making of the order, or any person claiming an interest (s. 86(5)). If it is not so discharged, a PRO ceases to have effect when the child reaches the age of 18 and it may terminate earlier where, for example, the child is adopted (s. 86(6)).

Further reading
E. E. Sutherland, *Child and Family Law* (T & T Clark, 1999), chap. 7
A. B. Wilkinson and K. McK. Norrie, *The Law of Parent and Child in Scotland* (2nd ed., W. Green, 1999), chap. 20

---

7. THE CHILDREN'S HEARINGS SYSTEM

The children's hearings system has now been operating in Scotland for just under 30 years. Resulting from the recommendations of the *Report of the Committee on Children and Young Persons* (1964) (the *Kilbrandon Report*), it is founded on three principles:

(a) that children who "were wronged" could be accommodated in the same system as "children who did wrong";
(b) that both groups of children should receive intervention in their lives, where appropriate, on the basis of "treatment";
(c) that while courts may be the appropriate forum in which to determine disputed facts, the decision on what to do for the child, thereafter, could be dealt with more effectively by panels of three lay persons.

While aspects of the hearings system have been criticised, examined and reformed, this remains the philosophy today. The Children (Scotland) Act 1995, which introduced the most recent reforms, now governs the way the system operates and references in this chapter are to that Act unless otherwise stated.

HOW THE SYSTEM WORKS

Management and organisation
While overall responsibility for the children's hearings system lies with the Secretary of State for Scotland (s. 42), it is organised through the Scottish Children's Reporter Administration (SCRA) and Children's Panel Advisory Committees (CPACs). SCRA appoints, employs and manages the deployment of individual reporters throughout Scotland. While the 1995 Act talks in terms of the responsibilities of the Principal Reporter, the chief executive of SCRA, the work is carried out on a day-to-day basis by the individual reporters. CPACs, appointed by each local authority, advise on the appointment of the panel members, the lay people who make decisions in individual cases.

How a child comes into the system
Reporters are central to the operation of the system, since it is their function to receive information about children who may be in need of compulsory measures of supervision, to investigate the case, to decide whether a hearing should be convened and, if so, to arrange a hearing (s. 53). Information comes from a variety of sources, with most referrals coming from the police and the local authority. However, anyone can raise their concerns with a reporter. In addition, the courts refer cases to the reporter (s. 54).

Having received a report it is the duty of the reporter to investigate the case and he or she will call upon other agencies, like the local authority, to provide additional information (s. 56). In order to justify a hearing, the reporter must be satisfied of two things:

(a) that there is a prima facie case establishing one of the grounds of referral (discussed below), and
(b) that compulsory measures of supervision may be necessary.

The grounds of referral
Section 52(2) of the 1995 Act uses the term "conditions" when indicating the *only* grounds on which a child can be referred to a children's hearing apart from direct references from a court. However, they are universally known as the "grounds of referral". They are that:

(a) *the child is beyond the control of any relevant person.*
(b) *the child is falling into bad associations or is exposed to moral danger.* This ground may be satisfied by the child's own conduct, like "hanging out with a bad crowd", or by conditions in the home, like the presence of drug addicts.
(c) *the child is likely due to a lack of parental care (i) to suffer unnecessarily; or (ii) to be impaired seriously in his or her health or development.* While the term "parental care" is used, the reference is to a lack of care by anyone responsible for the child,

whether a parent or not. It is not necessary that the lack of care should be motivated by their malice or indifference. For example, parental refusal to allow a child to be treated with blood products because they feared infection with HIV has been held to be sufficient (*Finlayson (Applicant)* (1989)).

(d) *the child is a child in respect of whom any offence mentioned in Schedule 1 to the Criminal Procedure (Scotland) Act 1995 has been committed.* Broadly, the specified offences are sexual offences, offences relating to child pornography, and offences suggesting neglect of the child (exposing the child to various hazards).

(e) *the child is, or is likely to become, a member of the same household as a child in respect of whom any of the offences referred to in paragraph (d) above has been committed.* This is simply a reference back to the ground above and enables all the children in a family to be considered where one child has been a victim of a specified offence.

(f) *the child is, or is likely to become, a member of the same household as a person who has committed any of the offences referred to in paragraph (d) above.* Again, this is a reference back to the specified offences and is designed to protect all children who might become part of the same household as the perpetrator of such an offence.

(g) *the child is, or is likely to become, a member of the same household as a person in respect of whom an offence under ss. 1–3 of the Criminal Law (Consolidation) (Scotland) Act 1995 (incest and intercourse with a child by a step-parent or a person in a position of trust) has been committed by a person in that household.* This again seeks to protect children who might become part of the same household as a particular type of victim who lives with an offender, in this case, a person convicted of incest or intercourse in breach of trust.

(h) *the child has failed to attend school regularly without reasonable excuse.* Since all children are required to receive the opportunity of education, truancy is a ground of referral, whether it is a matter of the child's choice or because a parent failed to send the child to school or make other appropriate arrangements.

(i) *the child has committed an offence.* Since Scots law sets the age of criminal responsibility at eight, only a child of this age or older can satisfy this ground (Criminal Procedure (Scotland) Act 1995, s. 41).

(j) *the child has misused alcohol or any drug, whether or not a controlled drug within the meaning of the Misuse of Drugs Act.* It should be noted that it is the *misuse*, rather than the use, of alcohol or drugs that is relevant here.

(k) *the child has misused a volatile substance by deliberately inhaling its vapour, other than for medicinal purposes.* This ground was introduced in 1983 to deal with the problem of "glue sniffing" and other misuse of volatile substances.

(l)   *the child is being provided with accommodation by a local author-*
       ity under section 25, or is the subject of a parental responsibilities
       order obtained under section 86, of this Act and, in either case, his
       or her behaviour is such that special measures are necessary for his
       or her adequate supervision in his or her interest or the interest of
       others. Where a local authority is looking after a child, it may be
       that the child's behaviour is such that the local authority believes
       additional measures, including the use of secure accommoda-
       tion, may be necessary in order to protect the child from his or
       her own actions or to protect others from the child's conduct.
       This ground enables such additional measures to be considered
       and, if necessary, authorised.

Arranging a hearing
Where the reporter is satisfied that there is a prima facie case establishing one or more of the grounds of referral *and* that compulsory
measures of supervision may be necessary (*i.e.* that other arrangements will not be sufficient), he or she will arrange a hearing. The
three panel members who will constitute the particular hearing will
be notified of the time, date and place of the hearing and will be provided with copies of the relevant background documents. "Relevant
persons" receive similar notification and, as a result of reforms introduced in response to criticism from the European Court of Human
Rights (*McMichael v. U.K.* (1995)), now also receive copies of the relevant documents (s. 45(8) and (9)). The child is entitled to receive
notification in writing of the time, date and place of the hearing and
of his or her right and obligation to attend (s. 45(1)), but does not
receive a full set of documents. Prior to the hearing, the reporter may
arrange a business meeting with three panel members to discuss procedural and other administrative matters (s. 64).

The hearing—those who may be present and their functions
The conduct of the hearing is a matter for the chairman of each
hearing and he or she is directed to permit attendance only by persons
whose presence is necessary for the proper consideration of the case
and to take all reasonable steps to keep the number of persons present
to a minimum (s. 43). However, certain persons have a right to attend
the particular hearing, others have a right to attend hearings generally, and yet others may attend with the permission of the chairman.
     The child and the relevant persons (often the child's parents) are
entitled, and usually obliged, to attend the hearing (s. 45). A genetic
father, who is not also a relevant person, has a right (but no obligation) to attend, provided that he is living with the child's mother.
Obviously, the three panel members selected to serve on a particular
hearing will be present, as will the reporter, since he or she is obliged
to make a record of the hearing. Any safeguarder appointed by the
hearing will usually be present. A safeguarder is an independent
person appointed by the children's hearing or a sheriff to protect and

promote the child's interests (s. 41). Given the local authority's duty to provide a social background report and to implement decisions of the hearing on any supervision requirement (s. 71), a social worker is usually present and is likely to participate in discussions. The child and each relevant person may be accompanied by a person to assist them at the hearing. While the representative may be legally qualified, the absence of legal aid to pay for representation at hearings means that lawyers rarely appear. The right of journalists to be present at a hearing is subject to the hearing's power to exclude them (s. 43(3) and (4)). Members of the Council on Tribunals, or its Scottish Council, have the right to attend a hearing, subject to the hearing's power to exclude them (s. 43(3) and (4)). A host of other persons may be permitted to attend a hearing at the chairman's discretion. The child's school teacher, for example, may have a valuable contribution to make and may be present.

The hearing—explaining the grounds of referral
The first thing the chairman of the hearing must do, after introducing those present and explaining the purpose of the hearing, is to explain the grounds of referral to the child and the relevant persons. Since it is only where the child and the relevant persons accept the grounds of referral that the hearing can proceed, this is of immense importance (s. 64(1)). The child and the relevant persons must then be asked if they accept the grounds of referral and, depending on their responses, various things can happen with different results.

If *the child does not understand* the grounds of referral, the hearing can either discharge the referral or direct the reporter to apply to the sheriff for a finding as to whether any of the grounds of referral is established (s. 65(9)). The decision is determined by the welfare principle (s. 16). Once discharged, no further action can be taken in relation to that ground of referral. Where the child or any of the relevant persons *do not accept the grounds of referral*, the hearing can, again, either discharge the referral or direct the reporter to apply to the sheriff for a finding as to whether any of the grounds of referral is established (s. 65(7)(a)). Where the child or the relevant persons *accept only part* of the grounds of referral, the hearing can proceed in respect of those grounds (s. 65(6)), or it can discharge the referral, or direct the reporter to apply to the sheriff for a finding as to whether any of the grounds of referral is established (s. 65(7)(b)). Where the child and the relevant persons *accept the grounds of referral as stated*, the hearing proceeds to the next stage (s. 65(5)). Throughout the proceedings of a children's hearing, the members must bear in mind that it may be necessary to appoint a safeguarder and, if so, to make such an appointment (s. 41).

Application to the sheriff
Where grounds of referral are not understood by the child or not accepted by the child or any of the relevant persons, the hearing may

direct the reporter to apply to the sheriff for a finding as to whether any of the grounds of referral are established. Where the reporter has lodged an application, it must be heard by the sheriff within 28 days (s. 68(2)). Proof is on the balance of probabilities, except where it is alleged that the child has committed an offence, in which case proof beyond reasonable doubt is required (s. 68(3)). The child is entitled and is usually obliged to attend the proof (s. 68(4) and (5)). Relevant persons also have a right to attend and the child and the relevant persons may be represented, with legal aid being available to fund representation (s. 68(4)). In addition, the sheriff must consider whether it is necessary to appoint a safeguarder for the child (s. 41).

Where the sheriff finds that none of the grounds of referral has been established, he or she must dismiss the application and discharge the referral (s. 8(9)). Where the sheriff finds any of the grounds of referral to have been established, he or she will remit the case back to the reporter to arrange for a hearing to determine the case (s. 68(10)(a)).

The hearing—consideration of the case

Where the grounds of referral are accepted by the child and the relevant persons or are established before the sheriff, the hearing moves on to consider the case. In the case of accepted grounds, the whole process will often be continuous. The hearing considers not only the grounds of referral but also any available reports, including social background reports, and other relevant information (s. 69(1)). It is of the essence of the hearings system that everyone involved should have the opportunity to participate freely in seeking a positive way forward for the child and the hearing is directed to discuss the case with the child, the relevant persons, any representative and any safeguarder.

Exclusion of a relevant person

The 1995 Act introduced the possibility of excluding a relevant person (s. 46), acknowledging that a child's right to participate in his or her own hearing might be inhibited by the presence of a particular adult. Exclusion is permitted in two situations: either it must be necessary in order to obtain the child's views; or the person's presence must be causing, or be likely to cause, significant distress to the child. A relevant person's representative may also be excluded from the hearing. Once the excluded person returns to the hearing, the chairman is obliged to explain to him or her the substance of what has taken place in his or her absence.

The hearing's decision

Having considered the case fully, the hearing will then decide on the appropriate disposal of the case. The disposal must be made in the light of the welfare principle and the following three options are open to the hearing:

Continue the case
The hearing may be continued to a later date, where, for example, the panel members require further information (s. 69(2)).

Discharge the referral
Unless the hearing is satisfied that the child is in need of compulsory measures of supervision it must discharge the referral and all orders, requirements and warrants issued in connection with the ground of referral so discharged cease to have effect (s. 69(1)(b), (12) and (13)).

Make a supervision requirement
Where the hearing is satisfied that the child is in need of compulsory measures of supervision, it will make a supervision requirement (s. 69(1)(c)). The nature of the supervision requirement is governed by the welfare principle (s. 16(1)). The child may be required to live at a specified place (s. 70(3)(a)). While a hearing may decide that a child should live with his or her parents, the power to require a child to live at a specified place is very wide-ranging indeed, and may mean that the child goes to live with other relatives, foster carers or in a residential establishment. The decision of a hearing supersedes any court order governing the child's residence (*Aitken v. Aitken* (1978)). The hearing has the power to impose any other condition that is consistent with the general principles of Part II of the 1995 Act (s. 70(3)(a)). Any condition must be stated in unambiguous language along with the reasons for its imposition. Punishment forms no part of the hearings system and conditions must be aimed at meeting the child's welfare needs.

While not limiting the range of conditions a hearing may make, the Act mentions two possible conditions. The first requires the child to submit to any medical examination or treatment (s. 70(5)(a)). However, the hearing has no power to impose a condition which would limit the child's general right to consent to or refuse such treatment, where the child is of sufficient maturity to understand what it involves (s. 90). The second condition mentioned allows the hearing to regulate the child's contact with any specified person or class of persons (s. 70(5)(b)). The hearing may also require that the place where the child is to live should not be disclosed to a specified person or class of persons (s. 70(6)) or require that the supervision requirement shall be reviewed at a particular time (s. 70(7)).

Appeals
Appeals from the decision of a children's hearing are infrequent. However, the child and any relevant person has standing to appeal, whether or not the person actually attended the hearing (s. 51(1)), as does the child's safeguarder. Legal aid is available to fund representation for an appeal. A genetic father, who is not also a relevant person, has no right to appeal. The reporter may not appeal against the decision of a hearing. The appeal must be lodged within three weeks,

beginning with the date of the hearing's decision (s. 51(1)) and the date assigned for hearing the appeal must be no more than 28 days after the appeal was lodged.

At the outset, and throughout the appeal, the sheriff must consider whether it is necessary to appoint a safeguarder (s. 41). The sheriff is directed to allow the appeal if he or she is satisfied that the hearing's decision is "not justified in all the circumstances of the case" (s. 51(5)). Since *all the circumstances of the case* are relevant, the sheriff is entitled to consider changes in circumstances which have occurred since the hearing. In considering the appeal, the sheriff may hear evidence from the parties or their representatives. In addition, he or she may examine the reporter, examine the compilers of any reports, and call for any further reports which may be of assistance (s. 51(3)).

Having heard all the evidence, the sheriff will allow or dismiss the appeal. If the appeal is dismissed, the sheriff must confirm the decision of the hearing (s. 51(4)). If the sheriff allows the appeal, he or she may remit the case back to the hearing, with reasons for allowing the appeal, so that the hearing can reconsider the case (s. 51(5)(c)(i)); or discharge the child from any further hearing in relation to the grounds of referral (s. 51(5)(c)(ii)); or substitute any disposal that the children's hearing could have made without any need to refer the case back to a hearing (s. 51(5)(c)(iii)).

Further appeal lies by way of stated case from the sheriff direct to the Court of Session or to the sheriff principal and, with leave from the sheriff principal, to the Court of Session, on a point of law or in respect of any irregularity in the conduct of the case (s. 51(11)). Such appeals are open to the child, any relevant person, the safeguarder, and the reporter on behalf of the children's hearing (s. 51(12)) and the application to state a case for the purpose of the appeal must be made within 28 days of the decision being made (s. 51(13)). There is no appeal to the House of Lords (s. 51(11)(b)).

Review of established grounds of referral—new evidence
Very occasionally, new evidence may emerge which casts doubt on grounds of referral which have been established. As a result of what came to be known as the *Ayrshire Case* (*L, Petitioners (No. 1) and (No. 2)* (1993)), the 1995 Act introduced a provision for dealing with new evidence relating to the grounds of referral which is available in the following, very limited, circumstances:

(a) challenging established grounds of referral is available only to the child and the relevant persons (s. 85(4));
(b) the grounds under challenge must have been established before the sheriff (s. 85(2));
(c) the applicant must claim (i) to have evidence which was not considered by the sheriff in the original application and which might have materially affected that application; (ii) that this evidence is

likely to be credible and reliable and would have been admissible in respect of the original application; and (iii) that there is a reasonable explanation of the failure to lead the evidence during the original application (s. 85(3)).

If the sheriff is not satisfied that the claims made are established, he or she must dismiss the application and the hearing's disposal stands (s. 85(5)). Where the sheriff is satisfied that the claims made in the application for review are established, there are two possibilities. Either, the challenge is such that all of the grounds of referral are struck down by it, or, while some of the grounds are no longer established, others remain valid. Where any ground of referral remains established, the sheriff may remit the case to the reporter to arrange a hearing and, pending the hearing, may order that the child be kept in a place of safety (s. 85(6)(b)). Where none of the original grounds remain established there is no longer any valid reason for a supervision requirement unless new grounds are established (s. 85(7)(b)). However, the Act acknowledges that it might be precipitate simply to return the child to the family without any arrangements for transition. Thus, while the sheriff may terminate the supervision requirement immediately, he or she may also postpone such termination (s. 85(7)(a)).

Review of the supervision requirement
Unless a supervision requirement is reviewed within one year of its being made, it ceases to have effect (s. 73(2)). Where a child is subject to a supervision requirement, the local authority must refer a case to the reporter for review where it is satisfied, either, that the requirement ought to cease to have effect or be varied or that a condition contained in the requirement is not being complied with; or the best interests of the child would be served by their applying for a parental responsibilities order, applying for an order freeing the child for adoption, or placing the child for adoption (s. 73(4)). The child or any relevant person may apply for review of a supervision requirement at any time three months after, either, the date when the requirement was made or the date of the most recent continuation or review of a requirement (s. 73(6)).

A hearing to review a supervision requirement operates much like the original hearing and can continue the review hearing to allow for further investigation, terminate the supervision requirement, vary the requirement, insert in the requirement any other requirement it could have made, or continue the requirement (s. 73(9)).

Further reading
K. McK. Norrie, *Children's Hearings in Scotland* (W. Green, 1997)
E. E. Sutherland, *Child and Family Law* (T & T Clark, 1999), chap. 9
A. B. Wilkinson and K. McK. Norrie, *The Law of Parent and Child in Scotland* (2nd ed., W. Green, 1999), chap. 19

8. COHABITING AND GETTING MARRIED

Adults live in many different kinds of relationships. While marriage is less popular than it was in the past, a little under 30,000 couples get married in Scotland each year. Cohabitation outside marriage has increased in popularity, either as a precursor, or alternative, to marriage, with couples being more open about the nature of the relationship than they were in the past. Cohabitation by same-sex couples is increasingly open and accepted. Nonetheless, the legal system still lays down clear rules for marriage and, as we shall see in chapter 9, attaches consequences to it. Where cohabitation is recognised as having consequences, the law again indicates which relationships it will accept as falling within that category. The Scottish Law Commission's modest recommendations for change in respect of heterosexual cohabitants (*Report on Family Law* (1992)) have not been implemented and are being discussed afresh (*Improving Scottish Family Law* (1999)). Thus, we may see some changes in the near future.

COHABITATION

Cohabitation is the state in which a couple live together quite openly, without any pretence that they are, in fact, married. One difficulty the legal system has with cohabitation is how to define it. How long do the parties have to live together before they are regarded as cohabiting? What should be their level of commitment? Does it matter whether they have children? As we will see in chapter 9, where the law does recognise cohabitation for a particular purpose, like the right to live in the family home, it couches its definition in terms of a heterosexual marriage-like relationship. A second problem arises over the reasons why people cohabit. Given that some couples cohabit as an express rejection of the concept of marriage, should their choice be respected by allowing them to avoid the consequences of marriage? Is that fair to couples who have lived together for a long time and had children? There is little legal regulation of who may cohabit, apart from the general provisions of the criminal law which outlaw certain types of incestuous sexual relationships. There are no formalities to be observed for a couple to cohabit.

IRREGULAR MARRIAGE

The expression "common law marriage" is used somewhat loosely and erroneously, in lay circles and the media, to denote a cohabitation relationship. However, Scots law still recognises one form of irregular marriage—marriage by cohabitation with habit and repute. Since it requires no statutory formalities, it can accurately be described as common law marriage. For a valid marriage by cohabitation with habit and repute to exist, all of the following conditions must be satisfied:

(a) The couple must live together *as husband and wife*, rather than as lovers, employer and housekeeper, or what the older cases describe as "man and mistress".

(b) The cohabitation must be *in Scotland*.

(c) The cohabitation must be for *a sufficiently long time*. It has been emphasised consistently that there is no hard and fast rule and that the quality of the cohabitation and repute are what matters. The more recent cases have accepted periods of cohabitation of less than a year as being sufficient (*Shaw v. Henderson* (1982) (11 months); *Mullen v. Mullen* (1991) (six months)).

(d) The parties must be *reputed to be husband and wife* and "although repute need not be universal it must be general, substantially unvarying and consistent and not divided" (*Low v. Gorman* (1970), p. 359).

(e) The parties must have *capacity to marry*. If there was an impediment, like a pre-existing marriage, at the beginning of the cohabitation, but that has now been removed by divorce, the clock can begin to run from the date of the divorce (*Shaw v. Henderson* (1982)).

Where such a marriage is claimed to exist, it is usual to seek a declarator of marriage in the Court of Session. Sometimes this is sought after the death of one of the parties in order that the survivor can claim succession rights. Once recognised, such a marriage has all the effects of a regular marriage. Marriage by cohabitation with habit and repute is now very rare and the concept has been criticised for rewarding deceptions and creating uncertainty. The Scottish Law Commission recommended its prospective abolition (*Report on Family Law* (1992), Rec. 42).

ENGAGEMENT TO MARRY

Actions for breach of promise of marriage were abolished in 1984 (Law Reform (Husband and Wife) (Scotland) Act 1984, s. 1(1)). However, where property was transferred by one party to the other in contemplation of marriage, such property can be recovered if the marriage does not take place (*Shilliday v. Smith* (1998)). Engagement rings have presented a particular problem where the marriage has not gone ahead. In one case, the court regarded the ring as an unconditional gift, and the woman was allowed to keep it (*Gold v. Hume* (1950)), while in another case, it was treated as a conditional gift, and the man who had given it was entitled to get it back (*Savage v. McAllister* (1952)).

REGULAR MARRIAGE—RESTRICTIONS

Since the legal system has always treated marriage as being important, there is extensive regulation of who may marry. Some restrictions can

be seen to protect the individuals. Thus, a marriage may be void where
one of the parties was coerced into entering it. Other restrictions, like
the prohibition on marriage between people who are closely related,
express a more general, societal, interest in marriage. The main statute
governing marriage is the Marriage (Scotland) Act 1977 and references in this chapter are to that Act unless otherwise stated.

Age

The 1977 Act takes a two-pronged approach to the issue of age. First,
it provides that no person domiciled in Scotland may marry before
reaching the age of 16, regardless of where the marriage takes place
(s. 1(1)). Domicile is the link between an individual and a legal system
and where a domiciled Scot goes through a ceremony of marriage
abroad before his or her sixteenth birthday, the marriage will not be
recognised here, regardless of what the law might permit in the other
country. Secondly, the 1977 Act provides that a marriage solemnised
in Scotland, where either of the parties is under 16, shall be void (s.
1(2)). Once a person reaches the age of 16, he or she has the capacity
to marry and parental consent (or opposition) is irrelevant.

Male and female

For a valid marriage, the parties must be respectively male and
female. A purported marriage between parties of the same sex will be
void (s. 5(4)(e)). Scots law, unlike some other legal systems, does not
recognise the possibility of a person changing sex, regardless of
whether the change occurs naturally (*X, Petitioner* (1957)) or is
brought about by surgical or other intervention (*Corbett v. Corbett*
(1971)). Whether the legal system should permit same-sex marriage
or, at least, accord some recognition to such relationships, is a
popular topic of debate and greater attention will undoubtedly be
given to the matter in the future.

Prior subsisting marriage

The starting point is that only monogamous marriage is recognised
in Scotland, that is, a person may only be married to one spouse at a
time. Where one party is already married, any subsequent attempt at
marriage is void (s. 5(4)(b)). Furthermore, anyone who attempts to
marry again, in the knowledge that a prior marriage remains valid,
commits the offence of bigamy. Where one of the parties to a big-
amous marriage was unaware of his or her partner's prior subsisting
marriage, the second ceremony creates what is known as a "putative
marriage". This is not a marriage in any real sense, but a child born
as a result of such a union is deemed in law to be legitimate. As
Scotland became more culturally diverse, the issue of polygamy
(usually, a man having more than one wife simultaneously) arose.
Initially, Scots law did not recognise polygamous marriages
(*Muhammad v. Suna* (1956)). Statute intervened long ago to provide
recognition of such marriages in certain circumstances (Matrimonial

Proceedings (Polygamous Marriages) Act 1972 and the Private International Law (Miscellaneous Provisions) Act 1995, s. 7(2)).

Prohibited degrees of relationship

A purported marriage between persons who are closely related to each other is void. Originally, the prohibitions were derived from the *Old Testament* (Leviticus, xviii, 6–24) and reinforced by the belief that procreation by close relatives increases the likelihood of genetic defects being passed on to future generations. The modern prohibitions are now contained exclusively in section 2 of and Schedule 1 to the 1977 Act, as amended; that is, if a marriage is not within the degrees specified there, it is permitted. Marriage is not allowed between persons who are regarded as being too closely related to each other by reason of a blood relationship (consanguinity), a family relationship through marriage (affinity), or a relationship created by adoption. In some cases, where marriage is within the prohibited degrees, sexual intercourse between the parties would amount to the offence of incest (*e.g.* father/daughter), while in others it would not (*e.g.* son-in-law/mother-in-law). Clive gives the following succinct explanation of the detailed prohibitions set out in the Act:

"You cannot marry (a) your parent, grandparent or great grandparent; (b) your child, grandchild or great grandchild; (c) your brother, sister, nephew, niece, uncle or aunt. Relations of the half blood are treated in the same way as relations of the full blood. These are the only blood relations with whom marriage is prohibited. So you can marry your cousin or a remoter relative . . . You cannot marry your former spouse's child or grandchild (or—to put it the other way round—the former spouse of your parent or grandparent), unless: (a) you have both attained the age of 21; and (b) "the younger party has not at any time before attaining the age of 18 lived in the same household as the other party and been treated by the other party as a child of the family . . . You cannot marry your former spouse's parent unless: (a) you have both attained the age of 21, and (b) your former spouse and his or her other parent are both dead.

There is a corresponding restriction on marriage to the former spouse of your child—which is, of course, just the same prohibition expressed the other way round.

The above are the only prohibitions based on affinity. It follows that you can marry your former spouse's brother, sister, nephew, niece, uncle, aunt or grandparent . . . You cannot marry your adoptive parent or former adoptive parent, or your adopted child or former adopted child. These are the only prohibitions based on adoption. It follows that you can marry your brother or sister by adoption, provided that no other prohibition applies. (E. M. Clive, *The Law of Husband and Wife in Scotland* (4th ed., 1997, W. Green), at paras 3.006–3.011, footnotes omitted.)

Consent

Marriage is a consensual relationship, that is, each party should consent freely and with full understanding of what he or she is doing. Where that consent is sufficiently impaired by, for example, insanity or coercion, the marriage will be void. The following examples illustrate how consent may be impaired.

Mental illness or defect

Where one of the parties is incapable, by reason of mental illness or defect, of understanding the nature of the marriage ceremony or of giving consent to marriage, the marriage is void. However, in *Long v. Long* (1950), a young woman was found to be of limited intelligence but still quite capable of understanding the nature of marriage and of consenting to it. The court made clear that a heavy burden of proof lies on the person seeking to challenge the validity of a marriage.

Intoxication

Where an individual's capacity to consent is sufficiently affected by the consumption of alcohol or drugs that he or she does not understand the nature of the ceremony the marriage will be void. It is thought that the intoxicated person is required to challenge the validity of the marriage on regaining his or her senses.

Error and fraud

After marriage, people sometimes find that a partner is not as they expected. However, only a very limited range of serious errors surrounding marriage will render the marriage void. Error as to the nature of the ceremony or the identity of the other party will have this effect. For example, where a person believed the ceremony to be one of engagement, rather than marriage, the marriage will be void. Similarly, if a man believed he was marrying one identical twin and, in fact, went through the ceremony with the other, the marriage would be void. Error as to other factors, such as the qualities of the spouse or what life after the marriage will be like, do not vitiate a marriage. This is so even where the error results from the other party's fraud. Thus, in *Lang v. Lang* (1921), where a woman induced a man to marry her by telling him that he was the father of the child she was expecting, he was unable to reduce the marriage on discovering that she had lied.

Duress and force and fear

In order to invalidate a marriage, the duress or pressure exerted on the party must have had the effect of making the individual appear to consent when he or she would not have done so but for the influence being exerted. Threat or pressure are not confined to physical harm to the individual consenting and can include the threat of imprisonment, social ostracism or harm to another person. While family members putting pressure on a reluctant young woman to go through with an arranged marriage she did not want would, itself, have been insufficient, the court accepted that this pressure, combined with threats to disown her, cut her off financially and send her to live in Pakistan, was sufficient to vitiate her consent and the marriage was declared void (*Mahmood v. Mahmood* (1993). See also, *Mahmud v. Mahmud* (1994)).

Sham marriages
Where the parties go through what seems to be a valid ceremony of marriage, but it can be established that there was "no true matrimonial consent and that the ceremony was only designed as a sham", then the marriage will be void (*Orlandi v. Castelli* (1961), at p. 120). Avoiding immigration requirements is a common motive for such "marriages".

Unilateral mental reservation
Unlike sham marriages, where there are usually bilateral mental reservations, unilateral mental reservation arises where one party believes that he or she is getting married but the other party does not believe that a valid marriage will result from the ceremony. In *McLeod v. Adams* (1920), where apparently consenting was simply a part of the man's overall scheme to get access to the widow's money and abscond with it, she was able to have the marriage declared void.

Joke marriages
Where apparent consent to marriage is given in the context of a joke, there is no true consent to marriage and, thus, no marriage (*Dunn v. Dunn's Trustees* (1930)).

REGULAR MARRIAGE—FORMALITIES

By laying down formal requirements for marriage, the legal system can, again, be seen as protecting individuals at the same time as expressing a general societal interest in marriage. So, for example, the requirements relating to celebrants should reduce the risk of "shotgun weddings", and requirements relating to notice and registration enable accurate public records to be kept. Both civil and religious marriage ceremonies are provided for and the 1997 Act expanded the range of religions accommodated. The early formalities are the same for all marriages, with the nature of the marriage only becoming important at the stage of celebration.

Notice of intention to marry
Each party intending to marry must submit notice of intention to marry, using a standard form and known as the "marriage notice", to the district registrar in the district where the marriage is to be solemnised (s. 3(1)). Each marriage notice must be accompanied by:

(a)   the prescribed fee;
(b)   a copy of the individual's birth certificate;
(c)   where a person has been married before, by a copy of the decree dissolving the previous marriage or a copy of the previous spouse's death certificate (s. 3(1)); and
(d)   where a person is not domiciled in the United Kingdom and has not been resident here for at least two years, a "certificate of no known impediment" from the country of his or her domicile, "if practicable"(s. 3(5)).

If either party is unable to submit any of the required documents, he or she may make a declaration stating that fact and the reasons why it is impracticable for the relevant document to be produced. Where any document submitted to the district registrar is in a language other than English, a certified translation must be submitted along with it (s. 3(3)).

Marriage notice book and display on list of intended marriages
On receiving the marriage notice, the district registrar must enter the prescribed particulars in the marriage notice book (s. 4(1)) and enter the names of the parties and the proposed date of the marriage in a list which is displayed in a conspicuous place at the registration office and remains there until the date for the marriage has passed (s. 4(2)). Any person who claims that he or she might have reason to submit an objection to an intended marriage may inspect the marriage notice book, free of charge, at any time when the registration office is open for public business (s. 4(3)).

Objections to a proposed marriage
Prior to a marriage taking place, any person may submit an objection in writing to the district registrar (s. 5(1)). Minor errors, like the misspelling of a name, can be dealt with by the district registrar with the approval of the Registrar General (s. 5(2)(a)). Where the objection relates to a more serious matter, like a pre-existing marriage, the district registrar will inform the Registrar General and suspend issuing the marriage schedule, pending consideration of the objection (s. 5(2)(b)).

The marriage schedule
Once the district registrar has received a marriage notice from each of the parties and is satisfied that no impediment to the marriage exists, or has been so informed by the Registrar General, he or she will complete a marriage schedule (s. 6(1)). This document serves as the basis for registration of all regular marriages. Where the marriage is to be a civil one, the district registrar simply retains it until the ceremony. Where the marriage is to be a religious one, it is collected by one of the parties (s. 6(3)) and acts as authority for the celebrant to perform the marriage. Usually, the district registrar may not issue a marriage sched-

ule until 14 days have elapsed since the marriage notices were lodged, although the Registrar General may authorise the district registrar to issue the schedule on an earlier date, if good cause can be shown (s. 6(4)(a)). In addition, the schedule will not normally be issued more than seven days before the ceremony is due to take place, but, again, the Registrar General may waive this requirement (s. 6(4)(a)).

Civil marriage
Only district registrars or assistant district registrars appointed by the Registrar General may solemnise a civil marriage and usually the ceremony must take place at the registration office (ss. 8(1)(b) and 17). However, a registrar may solemnise a marriage at another location within his or her registration district or, with the permission of the Registrar General, in another registration district, where there is no authorised registrar in certain, very limited, circumstances (s. 18(3)). If the registrar is satisfied that the party is unable to attend at his office because of serious illness or serious bodily injury and that there is good reason why the marriage cannot be delayed until the person can so attend, then he or she can perform the ceremony elsewhere (s. 18(4)(b)).

For a valid civil marriage the following persons must be present:

(a) both parties intending to marry;
(b) two witnesses "professing to be 16 years of age or over"; and
(c) the registrar.

The registrar must have the marriage schedule and the prescribed fee must have been paid (s. 19). The registrar explains the nature of the proceedings and impediments to marriage, establishes that the parties know of no such impediments and accept each other as spouses and declares them to be married. After the various declarations have been made, the parties, the witnesses and the celebrant sign the marriage schedule (s. 19(3)) and the particulars are entered in the register of marriages (s. 19(4)).

Religious marriage
A religious marriage can be solemnised by a person who is:

(a) a minister of the Church of Scotland; or
(b) a minister, clergyman, pastor, priest or other marriage celebrant of a religious body prescribed by regulations made by the Secretary of State; or
(c) nominated by some other body as a marriage celebrant and registered as such by the Registrar General under section 9 of the Act; or
(d) temporarily authorised by the Registrar General under section 12 of the Act (s. 8(1)(a)).

The ceremony should be performed on the date and at the place specified in the marriage schedule and there is provision for the district registrar to accommodate any change in plans after the schedule has been issued (s. 6(5)–(7)). Again, the parties intending to marry, two witnesses "professing to be 16 years of age or over", and the celebrant must be present and the celebrant have been given the marriage schedule (s. 13(1)). The celebrant must use a form of ceremony recognised by the relevant religious body and must include a declaration by the parties, in the presence of each other and two witnesses, that they accept each other as husband and wife and a declaration by the celebrant, thereafter, that they are husband and wife (s. 14). Nothing in the ceremony must be inconsistent with these declarations. Immediately after the marriage has been solemnised, the parties, the witnesses and the celebrant sign the marriage schedule (s. 15(1)). Within three days the parties must deliver the marriage schedule to the registrar or arrange for its delivery (s. 15(2)) and, on receipt, the registrar will enter the particulars in the register of marriages (s. 15(3)).

Non-compliance with formalities

The 1977 Act makes clear that failure to comply with certain fundamental requirements, like both parties being at least 16 years old, will render a marriage void. However, non-compliance with the more formal requirements will not invalidate a marriage provided that both parties were present at the ceremony and that the marriage has been registered (s. 23A). Thus, where these conditions are met, the validity of a marriage cannot be questioned simply because the celebrant was not authorised or one of the witnesses was under age.

Offences

Section 23A does not affect criminal liability. The 1977 Act provides that various kinds of conduct will constitute offences. These are set out in section 24 and cover such matters as falsification of documents, conducting a marriage ceremony when not authorised to do so and failing to register a marriage.

NON-MARRIAGE AND VOID AND VOIDABLE MARRIAGES

Certain impediments will render a marriage void. These relate to:

(a) either party being under the age of 16;
(b) the parties being within the prohibited degrees;
(c) the parties being of the same sex; or
(d) there being a lack of true consent to marriage on the part of either party.

Strictly speaking, a void marriage is not a marriage at all. However, since there will usually have been a ceremony and registration of the marriage, any person wishing to challenge such a "marriage" should raise an action for declarator of nullity of marriage at the Court of

Session. Either party may seek declarator as may anyone with a legitimate interest and such a declarator can be sought after the death of one of the parties (*Scott v. Kelly* (1992)). While, as a general rule, a void marriage is treated as not having taken place, there are exceptions. For example, when a court grants decree of declarator of nullity, it has the same powers to make financial provision as it has in granting decree of divorce (Family Law (Scotland) Act 1985, s. 17(3)).

The only ground on which a marriage is voidable is that one of the parties was incurably and permanently impotent at the time of the marriage; that is, he or she is unable (whether for physical or psychological reasons) to have full sexual intercourse. Only the parties to a voidable marriage have title to sue and a party may found on his or her own impotency (*F v. F* (1945)). The parties themselves may be personally barred from raising the action where, for example, they have adopted a child (*AB v. CB* (1961)). A voidable marriage remains valid until declarator of nullity is granted, whereupon the decree has retrospective effect. Again, the court may make financial provision. The Scottish Law Commission has recommended that the concept of voidable marriage should be abolished (*Report on Family Law*, Recs 49 and 50).

Further reading
E. M. Clive, *The Law of Husband and Wife in Scotland* (4th ed., W. Green, 1997), chaps 2–9
E. E. Sutherland, *Child and Family Law* (T & T Clark, 1999), chap. 10

---

9. THE CONSEQUENCES OF COHABITATION AND MARRIAGE

While marriage has fewer consequences for individuals than it did in the past, a number of significant effects still attach to it. Occasionally, these effects are extended to heterosexual cohabitants. In this chapter, we will examine the effects of marriage and cohabitation during the relationship. The financial consequences of a marriage ending, either by divorce or death, are discussed in chapter 11.

PERSONAL CONSEQUENCES

Name
The principle that "[a]ny person in Scotland may, without leave of the Court call himself what he pleases" (*Johnston, Petitioner* (1899)) applies to both men and women, with the caveat that the choice of name will fall foul of the law if it is used for a fraudulent purpose. It

follows that the convention which leads some married women to adopt their husband's surname on marriage is no more than a social convention. Married and cohabiting people may change their surnames or not as they wish.

Residence

While actions of adherence were abolished in 1984 (Law Reform (Husband and Wife) (Scotland) Act 1984, s. 2(1)), where one spouse refuses to live with the other without reasonable cause, such conduct entitles the latter to seek divorce for desertion after a period of two years. However, since the husband's right to choose the place of the matrimonial home was abolished by the same statute (1984 Act, s. 4), each spouse has an equal right to decide where they should live. If they cannot agree then, arguably, neither or both may be in desertion.

Children

The most significant consequence of marriage, for fathers, is that it gives them parental responsibilities and rights in respect of their children which they would not have in the absence of a court order or an agreement with the mother (Children (Scotland) Act 1995, ss. 3 and 4). As a general rule, only unmarried adults and married couples can adopt a child (Adoption (Scotland) Act 1978, ss. 14 and 15).

Remarriage and cohabitation

A married person cannot enter into another marriage while the first marriage remains in existence (Marriage (Scotland) Act 1977, s. 5(4)(b)). Once the first marriage is dissolved by divorce or the death of a spouse, individuals are free to remarry, but marriage to certain relatives of a former spouse is restricted or prohibited (1977 Act, s. 2 and Sched. 1). While a married person is not prevented from cohabiting with someone other than his or her spouse, such a relationship will almost certainly be grounds for divorce. Where a couple's relationship is one of unmarried cohabitation, either party may cohabit with, or marry, a new partner.

Sexual relations

Incurable impotence makes a marriage voidable and wilful refusal to have sexual relations may justify divorce. Adultery is a ground for divorce. While homosexual relations do not amount to adultery, such conduct will almost certainly justify the non-participating spouse in seeking a divorce. At one time, the law took the view that a husband could not rape his wife, since she had consented to sexual intercourse on marriage and, in any event, spouses were viewed as one person for most legal purposes. A series of cases, culminating in *S v. H.M. Advocate* (1989), where the parties were living together, put paid to this notion. In the words of Lord Justice-General Emslie, "Nowadays it cannot seriously be maintained that by marriage a wife submits herself irrevocably to sexual intercourse in all circumstances" (at p. 473).

Domicile, nationality and immigration
Domicile, the link between an individual and a legal system, can be particularly important for personal purposes like the capacity to marry and succession to moveable property. Increasingly, ordinary or habitual residence is now used as the connecting factor for civil purposes. Marriage no longer has any effect on a person's domicile (Domicile and Matrimonial Proceedings Act 1973, s. 1). While marriage has no automatic effect on either spouse's nationality, the foreign spouse of a British citizen can acquire nationality by naturalisation more easily than can other persons, based on residence for three years (British Nationality Act 1981, s. 6). Cohabitation has no effect on nationality. Marriage is important for immigration purposes, with foreign spouses and those engaged to be married gaining entry more easily than is the case ordinarily. While these rules do not apply to cohabitants, they are admitted on a discretionary basis. Nationals of Member States of the European Economic Area and their spouses are not governed by these rules and can enter and stay in the United Kingdom more easily.

CONTRACT AND DELICT

Contract
A host of sexist common law provisions, including the husband's guardianship of a young wife, the presumption that a wife was her husband's domestic manager and, thus, his agent, and the husband's liability for his wife's ante-nuptial debts, were abolished by the Law Reform (Husband and Wife) (Scotland) Act 1984. The Family Law (Scotland) Act 1985 sums up the present law, that is, that marriage "shall not of itself affect . . . the legal capacity of the parties" (s. 24(1)(b)). Thus, spouses have the same contractual capacity as all other people. However, the decision in *Smith v. Bank of Scotland* (1996) places an important qualification on that general rule. Ms Smith had granted a standard security to the bank over the matrimonial home, which she co-owned with her husband, so that he could obtain additional finance for his troubled business. When the bank sought to realise the security, Ms Smith raised an action of reduction alleging that she had granted the security due to the undue influence exerted and misrepresentations made by her husband, and that the bank could be regarded as having constructive knowledge of this conduct. While the Inner House rejected her claim, it was upheld by the House of Lords. Thus, anyone dealing with a spouse, at least in the context of cautionary obligations, may be deemed to know of the other spouse's undue influence or misrepresentation and similar knowledge may apply in the context of cohabitants.

Delict
At common law, spouses could not sue each other in delict, partly because the spouses were viewed as one, but also because such an action would not usually bring an overall financial gain to the family

unit. Statute intervened in 1962 to permit actions in delict between spouses (Law Reform (Husband and Wife) Act 1962, s. 2(1)), subject to the qualification that the court has the power to dismiss the action where "no substantial benefit would accrue to either party" (1962 Act, s. 2(2)). In practice, actions between spouses are not dismissed on this basis and, effectively, spouses can sue each other as if they were strangers. Spouses have no automatic liability for each other's delictual conduct, nor do cohabitants.

One spouse may claim damages in respect of the death of the other for: loss of support; distress and anxiety caused by contemplating the deceased's suffering prior to death; grief and sorrow caused by the deceased's death; the loss of the deceased's society and guidance; and funeral expenses (Damages (Scotland) Act 1976, s. 1). In addition, the surviving spouse may claim for loss of the deceased's services (Administration of Justice Act 1982, s. 9). A surviving cohabitant has similar claims provided that he or she was living with the deceased "as husband or wife" immediately prior to the deceased's death (Administration of Justice Act 1982, s. 14(4)). In addition to any claim he or she may have, a surviving spouse may also be the deceased's executor. If the deceased survived the delictual event and died later as a result of his or her injuries, the deceased's right of action now transmits to his or her executors, who may raise an action for damages or continue any action the deceased had time to raise (Administration of Justice Act 1982, s. 2). Where a spouse or partner is injured and survives, recovery is also possible for services rendered to the injured person by a partner or relative as a result of the injuries sustained and to compensate for services which the injured person can no longer provide to a partner or other relative (Administration of Justice Act 1982, ss. 7–9).

PROPERTY

The general position
At common law, on marriage, a husband became the owner of virtually all of his wife's moveable property and administrator of her heritable property. For this reason, ante-nuptial marriage contracts were popular amongst the wealthy. From the mid-nineteenth century, statute whittled away at the husband's dominant role and now the position is that "marriage shall not of itself affect the respective rights of the parties to the marriage in relation to their property" (Family Law (Scotland) Act 1985, s. 24(1)(a)). Thus, as a general rule, spouses are treated like strangers when it comes to property. However, this general rule is subject to a number of qualifications. The fact that two people are spouses can have an impact on their property, since spouses are obliged to aliment each other. If spouses divorce a whole legal regime applies to their property. On the death of one spouse, the surviving spouse has certain succession rights. In addition, the law recognises that couples will often arrange their lives differently from strangers and lays down a number of presumptions about the owner-

ship of certain kinds of property which is most likely to be held by a married couple. Perhaps the most striking exception to the separate property rule is the treatment of the family home and this is discussed at the end of this chapter.

The presumptions

The Family Law (Scotland) Act 1985 created a number of presumptions about the ownership of the most common household property. It should be remembered that these are simply presumptions and they can be rebutted by evidence. Where any property falls outwith the presumptions, disputed ownership will fall to be resolved according to the ordinary rules of property. The presumptions do not apply to cohabitants. The presumptions are as follows:

(a) *Household goods.* The 1995 Act creates a presumption that household goods are owned by the spouses in equal shares (s. 25(1)). "Household goods" are defined as goods "kept or used at any time during the marriage in any matrimonial home for the joint domestic purposes of the parties", but money and securities, cars and other road vehicles, and domestic pets are specifically excluded (s. 25(3)). The presumption applies to goods "acquired in contemplation of or during a marriage". However, it does not apply to goods acquired "by way of gift or succession from third parties" and so, for example, wedding presents given by friends will be outside its ambit.

(b) *Savings from housekeeping allowance.* Where a dispute arises over the ownership of "any allowance made by either party for their joint household expenses" or property derived from such an allowance, the money or property is treated as belonging to each party in equal shares, unless the parties have made an agreement to the contrary (s. 26). Thus, assuming nothing is said, where a husband buys a lottery ticket with the housekeeping allowance, any winnings belong to him and his wife in equal shares.

MONEY

Aliment

Each spouse owes an obligation to aliment the other (Family Law (Scotland) Act 1985, s. 1(1)(a) and (b)). The extent of the obligation is to provide such support as is reasonable in the circumstances, having regard to:

(a) the needs and resources of the parties;
(b) the earning capacities of the parties;
(c) generally all the circumstances of the case (s. 4(1)).

In chapter 5, we saw that these criteria applied to the obligation to aliment a child and the same principles apply, with allowance being made for the fact that adults are generally more able to provide for themselves. A party's conduct is irrelevant unless it would be "manifestly inequitable" to ignore it (s. 4(3)(b)). Claims for aliment are competent even where the parties are living in the same household (s. 2(6)), although it is a defence to a claim that they are so doing and the defender intends to continue to support the pursuer in this way (s. 2(7)). Where the parties are no longer living together, the defender may offer to receive the pursuer into his or her own household and provide aliment there. Such an offer only constitutes a good defence where it would be reasonable to expect the claimant to accept the offer to be housed in the defender's household and, in particular, the court is directed to have regard to "any conduct, decree or other circumstances" (s. 2(8) and (9)). When considering a spouse's claim for aliment, the court has the same powers as it has when dealing with aliment for children (s. 3). It should be noted that the obligation to aliment a spouse terminates on divorce and the law on financial provision on divorce becomes relevant then. There is no alimentary obligation between cohabitants.

State benefits
In the context of non-contributory, income-related benefits, like income support, family credit and housing benefit, the family is seen as a unit, with resources being aggregated. Heterosexual cohabiting couples are treated in the same way as married couples. For contributory benefits, like incapacity benefit, widow's benefit and retirement pensions, marriage, as opposed to cohabitation, emerges as significant in calculating entitlement to benefit.

Taxation
Increasingly, marriage is becoming irrelevant for tax purposes, a trend which will be continued with the abolition of the married couple's allowance.

CRIMINAL LAW AND JUDICIAL PROCEEDINGS

Criminal law
As a general rule, spouses are treated no differently from strangers and, thus, spouses can steal from one another (*Harper v. Adair* (1945)) and a husband can rape his wife (*S v. H.M. Advocate* (1989)). Special measures are available to combat the problem of domestic violence, although these are in addition to the possibility of prosecution for assault under the ordinary criminal law.

In addition, an adult relationship may be particularly relevant to other offences. Bigamy is an obvious example, since it is committed where a married person goes through a second ceremony of marriage while the first marriage is still in existence. Where marriage or cohabitation brings a person into a quasi-parental relationship with a child, the law recognises the potential for sexual exploitation of the child.

Thus, the Criminal Law Consolidation (Scotland) Act 1995 provides that it is an offence for a step-parent or former step-parent to have sexual intercourse with a step-child or former step-child, in certain circumstances (s. 2). Non-marital cohabitants are covered by an offence relating to intercourse where the adult was in a position of trust in respect of the child (s. 3).

Giving evidence—criminal cases

One spouse is a competent witness against the other in criminal proceedings; that is, he or she may give evidence (Criminal Procedure (Scotland) Act 1995, s. 264(1)). However, a spouse cannot be compelled to give evidence, unless that spouse was the victim of the alleged crime or was injured by it (1995 Act, s. 264(2)(a)). Nor can a spouse be compelled to disclose any communication made between the spouses during marriage (1995 Act, s. 264(2)(b)). Neither the prosecution nor the defence may comment upon a spouse's failure to give evidence (1995 Act, s. 264(3)). Cohabitants are both competent and compellable witnesses against each other.

Giving evidence—civil cases

While there is some debate on the matter, it is probably the case that spouses are both competent and compellable witnesses against each other in civil proceedings subject to an exemption in respect of confidential communications (Evidence (Scotland) Act 1853, s. 3). While it is competent for a spouse to give evidence relating to whether sexual intercourse took place between the couple, he or she cannot be compelled to do so (Law Reform (Miscellaneous Provisions) Act 1949, s. 7(2)). Former spouses do not appear to be protected from giving evidence against each other, nor are cohabitants.

THE MATRIMONIAL OR FAMILY HOME

At common law, one result of the separate property rule was that, where a spouse owned or was the sole tenant of the home, he could evict his partner at will (*Millar v. Millar* (1940)). During the 1970s, increased attention focused on the problems of domestic violence and how the law could be improved to protect the victims. Resulting from the work of the Scottish Law Commission (*Report on Occupancy Rights in the Matrimonial Home and Domestic Violence* (1980)), the Matrimonial Homes (Family Protection) (Scotland) Act 1981 sought to address these problems. The Act does not affect ownership of the home but, rather, is concerned with the use of it. It applies to married couples and, to a more limited extent, to cohabitants. With the exception of the court's power to transfer a tenancy, the protection offered by the Act applies during marriage. The Act ceases to have effect on divorce, when the law on financial provision on divorce becomes relevant.

What is a "matrimonial home"?

A matrimonial home includes obvious residences, like houses or flats, as well as caravans or houseboats, where the home "has been provided or has been made available by one or both of the spouses as, or has become, a family residence" (s. 22). It includes ground or buildings attached to the home itself and "required for the amenity or convenience" of the home, like a garden. It does not matter which of the spouses acquired the property, or when, and a couple can have more than one matrimonial home, for example, a flat in town and a cottage in the country. Any home acquired by one spouse for his or her own use is not included under the Act. Similarly, where a separated spouse acquires a home for his or her use, separately from the other spouse, that home is not governed by the Act. Where one spouse provides a home for the other spouse to live in, with or without the children, the Outer House has held that such a home is not a matrimonial home (*McRobbie v. McRobbie* (1984)).

"Entitled" and "non-entitled" spouses

Central to the Act is the concept of "entitled" and "non-entitled" spouses. An entitled spouse is one who has a right to occupy the matrimonial home, whether because he or she is the owner or tenant or because he or she is allowed by a third party to occupy it (s. 1(1)). A spouse with no such right is a "non-entitled" spouse. Thus, where the wife bought the home and it has been used by the couple, she is the entitled spouse and her husband is the non-entitled spouse.

Occupancy rights

The 1981 Act gives the non-entitled spouse a right to live in the matrimonial home by providing that, if already living there, he or she has the right to continue to occupy it (s. 1(1)(a)), and, where the spouse is not in occupation, he or she has a right to enter and occupy it (s. 1(1)(b)). These rights can be exercised along with any child of the family (s. 1(1A)). A non-entitled spouse may renounce his or her occupancy rights but only in a particular home (*i.e.* there cannot be a blanket renunciation for all future homes), and the renunciation must be in writing and sworn before a notary (s. 1(5) and (6)).

Subsidiary and consequential matters

Simply having the right to live in the home might not be enough on its own and, for example, a landlord would be unlikely to permit continued occupation where the rent remained unpaid for some time and a home without any appliances or furniture would be of limited use. For the purpose of securing his or her occupancy rights, the non-entitled spouse is allowed to do a number of things, like paying the rent or mortgage and carrying out essential repairs, without the permission of the entitled spouse (s. 2(1)). The court may make an order apportioning expenditure between the spouse in respect of such payments (s. 2(3)). In addition, the court may authorise non-

essential repairs and apportion payments made in respect of them
(s. 2(4)).

Regulatory orders

Either spouse may apply to the court for an order regulating occupancy rights and associated matters. This part of the Act applies not
only where there is a non-entitled and an entitled spouse, but also
where the spouses are both entitled or permitted to occupy the home.
A regulatory order may:

(a) declare the applicant's occupancy rights;
(b) enforce the applicant's occupancy rights;
(c) restrict the non-applicant's occupancy rights;
(d) regulate the exercise of occupancy rights by either party (s. 3(1)).

The court is bound to declare occupancy rights, where they exist,
but has a discretion in granting the remaining orders. In exercising its
discretion, the court is directed by s. 3(3) to make such an order as
appears "just and reasonable having regard to all the circumstances
of the case, including":

(a) the conduct of the spouses in relation to each other and otherwise;
(b) the respective needs and financial resources of the spouses;
(c) the needs of any child of the family;
(d) the extent (if any) to which, (i) the matrimonial home, and (ii)
any relevant item of furniture and plenishings, is used in connection with a trade, business or profession of either spouse; and
(e) whether the entitled spouse offers or has offered to make available to the non-entitled spouse any suitable alternative accommodation.

As we shall see, these criteria are used again later in the Act. In addition, the court cannot make an order under section 3 where its effect
would be to exclude the entitled spouse from the home (section 3(5)),
since exclusion orders are dealt with in section 4.

Exclusion orders

The right to live in the home is of little value if the threat of domestic violence continues because the violent partner is also living there.
For this reason, the 1981 Act introduced the exclusion order, which
empowers a court to order a person to leave the matrimonial home,
regardless of his or her rights as owner, tenant or non-entitled spouse.
The court is directed that it

> "*shall* make an exclusion order if it appears that the making of
> such an order is *necessary* for the protection of the applicant or
> any child of the family from *any conduct or reasonably appre-
> hended conduct* of the non-applicant spouse which is or would be

injurious to the physical or mental health of the applicant or child" (s. 4(2)), emphasis added).

However, the court is also directed not to grant an exclusion order if it would be unjustified or unreasonable, having regard to all the circumstances of the case, including those set out in section 3(3) of the Act (s. 4(3)(a)).

Initially, judicial hostility to the Act meant that it was interpreted in a very restrictive way (*Bell v. Bell* (1983)), but the courts overcame these early problems and are now more willing to exclude an abuser from his or her home. Perhaps the clearest guidance on how the court should approach an application for an exclusion order was given by Lord Dunpark, when he said that the court should consider the following questions:

"1. What is the nature and quality of the alleged conduct?

2. Is the court satisfied that the conduct is likely to be repeated if cohabitation continues?

3. Has the conduct been or, if repeated would it be injurious to the physical or mental health of the applicant or to any child of the family?

4. If so, is the order sought necessary for the future protection of the physical or mental health of the applicant or child?" (*McCafferty v. McCafferty* (1986), at p.656).

Protection of occupancy rights against dealings

The value of occupancy rights would be greatly diminished if the entitled spouse could sell the home to a third party and the third party could then come along and evict the non-entitled spouse. For this reason, the Act contains provisions designed to protect the non-entitled spouse from the entitled spouse's dealings with third parties. The non-entitled spouse's rights under the Act cannot be prejudiced by the entitled spouse's dealings with the property (s. 6(1)(a)). Nor can a third party acquire a right to occupy the property as a result of such dealings (s. 6(1)(b)). However, no protection is offered against certain dealings, where, for example, they predate the Act or the marriage or where a third party purchaser, acting in good faith, obtains an affidavit from the seller, declaring that the subjects of the sale are not a matrimonial home in which a spouse of the seller has occupancy rights (s. 6(3)).

Protection where both spouses are entitled to occupy the home

Increasingly, spouses who buy their homes do so in joint names. This means that there is neither an entitled, nor a non-entitled, spouse. Each spouse will have the right to live in the home and neither can bring an action of ejection against the other (s. 4(7)). However, the court can still regulate occupancy under section 3 and grant exclusion orders under section 4. Where each spouse has a *pro indiviso* share in the property he or she can sell or mortgage his or her share and can apply for a decree of division and sale in order to force the sale of the whole property. However, the Act restricts the effects of such action.

Where one spouse sells his or her share in the home to a third party, the other spouse's occupancy right will not be affected, nor will the third party acquire a right of occupancy (s. 9(1)). While one spouse may still apply for a decree of division and sale, the court has a discretion to refuse the decree, to postpone it, or to grant it subject to conditions (s. 19). In reaching its decision, the court is directed to consider all the circumstances of the case, including the factors set out in section 3(3), the conduct of the parties, and whether the spouse bringing the actions has offered suitable alternative accommodation to the other spouse.

Tenancy transfer orders
Many spouses are joint tenants in their home while, in other cases, only one spouse is the tenant. In either case, the court can regulate occupancy under s. 3 and grant an exclusion order under section 4. In addition, it can transfer the tenancy from one spouse to the other (s. 13(1)) or, where both spouses are tenants, vest the tenancy in one of them alone (s. 13(9)) and provide for reasonable compensation to be paid to the deprived former tenant (s. 13(11)). In reaching its decision, the court is directed to consider all the circumstances of the case, including the factors in section 3(3), the applicant's suitability to become a tenant and the applicant's capacity to perform the obligations under the lease (s. 13(3)). A copy of the application must be served on the landlord who must be given an opportunity to be heard before the court grants the transfer (s. 13(4)), although the court can transfer tenancy even where the landlord does not agree (s. 13(6)). Certain kinds of tenancy, like a tied house, cannot be transferred by the court (s. 13(7) and (8)).

Matrimonial interdicts
In order to offer further protection against domestic violence, the 1981 Act took the traditional remedy of interdict, whereby the court orders a person not to do a particular thing, and "gave it teeth". "Matrimonial interdicts" relate to restraining the conduct of one spouse towards the other or a child of the family or prohibit the spouse from being in, or near to, the matrimonial home (s. 14(2)). The courts may, and in some circumstances must, attach a power of arrest to matrimonial interdicts (s. 15(1)) and, where this has been done, a police officer may arrest the interdicted spouse where there is reasonable cause to suspect that he or she is in breach of the interdict (s. 15(2)). Where the spouse is arrested, he or she will be taken to a police station, may be detained before being brought before the sheriff, and may be further detained for a period not exceeding two days (ss. 16 and 17). Thereafter, proceedings for breach of interdict may follow.

Cohabiting couples
The 1981 Act applies to "a man and woman who are living with each other as if they were man and wife" (s. 18(1)) and, in determining who

qualifies, the court is directed to consider all the circumstances of the case including the duration of the cohabitation and whether there are any children of the relationship (s. 18(2)). However, there are important differences between the way the Act applies to married couples and to cohabitants. The latter have no automatic occupancy rights and must apply to the court to be granted them. Initially, these may be granted for a period of up to six months and, thereafter, any number of extensions of up to six months each may be granted indefinitely (s. 18(1)). Where both partners are entitled to occupy the home, there is no need to apply for occupancy rights and the Act applies as if such rights had been granted (s. 18(3)). Where the partners have occupancy rights, most of the provisions of the Act can be used by them. For example, they can apply for regulatory orders (s. 3), exclusion orders (s. 4), tenancy transfer orders (s. 13), and matrimonial interdicts (s. 14). The protection against dealings afforded to spouses does not apply in the case of a cohabitant (s. 18(5)).

Debt, sequestration and the family home
The family home receives special protection in the context of bankruptcy under section 40 of the Bankruptcy (Scotland) Act 1985. The 1985 Act contains its own definitions which are not identical to those found in the 1981 Act and should be consulted for its terms. Essentially, it provides that the trustee in sequestration may not sell a family home without the consent of the debtor's spouse (or former spouse, if he or she is occupying the family home) or the permission of the court. The court may refuse the application, grant it subject to conditions or postpone the granting of it for up to a year.

The Debtors (Scotland) Act 1987, s. 16, recognises the importance of essential household items by exempting them from poinding where such goods are located in the dwellinghouse of the debtor and reasonably required for use there by the debtor or a member of his or her household. This provision *does* protect the household goods of a debtor living alone or with a cohabitant.

Further reading
E. M. Clive, *The Law of Husband and Wife in Scotland* (4th ed., W. Green, 1997), chaps 11–18

E. E. Sutherland, *Child and Family Law* (T & T Clark, 1999), chaps 11 and 12

---

10. DIVORCE

Divorce has been available in Scotland from the time of the Reformation, with adultery and desertion being the only grounds mentioned in the Act of 1573. Later statutes extended the grounds, but divorce remained firmly tied to the concept of fault, and only the "innocent spouse" could raise the action. It was not until the Divorce (Scotland) Act 1976 that the concept of no-fault divorce was recognised and what we now have is a mixed system, with divorce being available on the basis of both fault and non-cohabitation. The addition of periods of non-cohabitation (with or without the other spouse's consent) to the more traditional grounds of adultery, behaviour and desertion, represented a massive departure from the notion of fault inherent in the previous law. For the first time, couples who agreed that divorce was the correct solution for them were freed from the need to rake over past misdeeds. References in this chapter are to the 1976 Act unless otherwise stated. The Scottish Law Commission recommended modest reform of the grounds for divorce in 1989 (*Report on Reform of the Grounds of Divorce* (1989)) and, while its proposals have not been implemented, they are being discussed afresh (*Improving Scottish Family Law* (1999)). Thus, we may see some changes in the near future.

JUDICIAL SEPARATION

Judicial separation is another remedy available to an unhappy spouse and is granted on the same grounds as divorce (s. 4). It was more widely used in the past, when divorce was more difficult to obtain and was less socially acceptable. While it gives a judicial stamp of approval to the parties' separation, it does little to alter their legal position and, most significantly, does not free them to remarry. The remedy is little used today and the Scottish Law Commission has recommended its abolition (*Report on Family Law* (1992)).

Divorce and judicial separation apply only to married couples. Just as cohabitants required no formalities to form their relationship, they do not need to go through any formal procedure to end it. However, they may still have to resolve disputes over the future arrangements for their children and over property and may become involved in judicial proceedings in order to do so.

IRRETRIEVABLE BREAKDOWN

The 1976 Act provides that the *sole* ground on which decree of divorce will be granted is that the marriage "has broken down irretrievably" (s. 1(1)). This, apparently broad, ground is misleading in two respects. First, irretrievable breakdown can only be established by satisfying one of the five factual circumstances set out in the Act (s. 1(2)). Thus, if spouses cannot satisfy one of the five factual circumstances, they cannot get divorced, however irretrievable they believe the breakdown to be. Secondly, provided that the pursuer can establish one of the five factual situations, he or she will be entitled to decree, even if the marriage might be salvaged; that is, it has not broken down irretrievably. It is hardly surprising, then, that the five factual situations themselves have come to be known as the "grounds of divorce".

GROUNDS OF DIVORCE

Each of the five grounds of divorce is discussed below. There are some 12,000 divorces each year and the non-cohabitation (*i.e.* no fault) grounds now account for over half of them. However, behaviour remains popular as a basis for divorce, with the use of adultery and desertion waning. Proof of each ground is on the balance of probabilities (1976 Act, s. 1(6)).

Adultery
Irretrievable breakdown will be established if "since the date of the marriage the defender has committed adultery" (s. 1(2)(a)). Adultery is voluntary sexual intercourse with a person of the opposite sex who is not one's spouse. It is not adultery for a spouse to form a close association with a person of the opposite sex unless sexual intercourse is involved, nor does a lesbian or homosexual affair qualify. It is not adultery for a woman to have donor insemination without her husband's consent (*MacLennan v. MacLennan* (1958)). Since the act must be voluntary, a woman who is raped does not commit adultery (*Stewart v. Stewart* (1914)), although a married rapist does.
    The following defences apply in the context of adultery:

(a) *Lenocinium* (s. 1(3)). This occurs where the pursuer actively and seriously encourages the defender to commit adultery and this encouragement was the cause of the adultery (*Hunter v. Hunter* (1883), *per* Lord President Inglis at p. 365).
(b) Condonation (s. 1(3)). Essentially, condonation arises where the defender knows of the adultery and continues to live with the defender, thus amounting to legal forgiveness. The 1976 Act encourages couples to attempt reconciliation and, thus, a period of resumed cohabitation of up to three months is permitted without the defence of condonation arising (s. 2(2)). In addition, where the court believes there is a prospect of reconciliation and continues the case, no resumption of cohabitation during that time will bar an action for divorce (s. 2(1)).
(c) Collusion. This is "an agreement to permit a false case to be substantiated or to keep back a good defence" and is essentially a conspiracy between the parties.

Behaviour
Irretrievable breakdown will be established if "since the date of the marriage the defender has at any time behaved (whether or not as a

result of mental abnormality and whether such behaviour has been active or passive) in such a way that the pursuer cannot reasonably be expected to cohabit with the defender" (s. 1(2)(b)). Only behaviour *after* the marriage is relevant and a single act (*e.g.* of violence) may suffice. The behaviour can be *active or passive* and, while a person's condition may be involuntary, it may result in behaviour which is such that the pursuer cannot reasonably be expected to cohabit with the defender. Thus, where a person is suffering from schizophrenia, with the result that he stays in bed and shows no interest in the family, his conduct may qualify, if the impact on his or her spouse is sufficient (*Fullarton v. Fullarton* (1976)). The behaviour itself need not be reprehensible, since it is the effect it has on the pursuer that is relevant. So, for example, a do-it-yourself enthusiast who reduced the home to a building site for two years, with the intention of improving it, justified his wife in seeking a divorce (*O'Neill v. O'Neill* (1975)). Nor need the conduct be directed at the other spouse. Behaviour is the most flexible of all the grounds for divorce and may include the following: physical, verbal or economic abuse; neglectful conduct or indifference; certain kinds of sexual behaviour; obsessive behaviour; drunkenness or drug abuse; and certain kinds of criminal conduct.

Collusion is a defence to an action based on behaviour. There are no specific provisions on resumed cohabitation or reconciliation attempts in this context, although the court could continue the action where it believed there was the prospect of a reconciliation, and resumed cohabitation during this period would not bar the action for divorce (s. 2(1)).

Desertion

Irretrievable breakdown will be established if "the defender has wilfully and without reasonable cause deserted the pursuer; and during a continuous period of two years immediately succeeding the defender's desertion (i) there has been no cohabitation between the parties, and (ii) the pursuer has not refused a genuine and reasonable offer by the defender to adhere" (s. 1(2)(c)).

The defender's initial desertion must be *wilful* and so, for example, where a spouse is imprisoned, but intends to resume married life on release, his or her absence does not amount to desertion (*Rose v. Rose* (1964)). In addition, the departure must be directed at leaving the marriage and not for some other purpose. Thus, a woman who went to stay with her aunt on holiday was not in desertion initially. However, when she wrote to her husband three weeks later, indicating that she did not intend to return, she was (*Macaskill v. Macaskill* (1939)). While desertion usually involves one spouse leaving the home, such departure is not essential and the parties may remain under the same roof, but with one of them withdrawing from all the practical elements of cohabitation. If one spouse ejects the other or locks him or her out, it is the spouse who takes this action and, thus, ends the cohabitation, who is in desertion despite the fact that he or she may remain in the home (*McMillan v. McMillan* (1962)).

To what extent must the pursuer have been willing to live with the defender at the time of the initial desertion and subsequently? This caused considerable problems in the past but the current position is that the pursuer must have been willing to adhere at the time of desertion. Thereafter, there must be a period of two years' non-cohabitation during which the pursuer has not refused the defender's genuine and reasonable offer to adhere. If the defender makes no such offer, the pursuer's state of mind during the subsequent two-year period is irrelevant.

Desertion is only a ground for divorce where the defender has acted *without reasonable cause*. Anything that would amount to behaviour making it unreasonable to expect the pursuer to cohabit with the defender for the purpose of s. 1(2)(b) would constitute reasonable cause for non-adherence. In addition, lesser conduct and pre-marital conduct, like a woman inducing a man to marry her by claiming falsely that he was the father of the child she was expecting (*Hastings v. Hastings* (1941)), would suffice.

It is apparent, then, that the pursuer's refusal of a genuine and reasonable offer from the defender to adhere (*i.e.* live together), made within two years of the initial desertion, is a defence to an action based on desertion. Similarly, reasonable cause for non-adherence is a defence. Resumed cohabitation for up to three months (s. 2(3)), or during any continuation for a reconciliation attempt, ordered by the court (s. 2(1)), will not bar an action for desertion. However, the period of resumed cohabitation will not count towards the two-year period required to establish desertion (s. 2(4)).

Two years' non-cohabitation and the defender's consent

Irretrievable breakdown will be established if "there has been no cohabitation between the parties at any time during a continuous period of two years after the date of the marriage and immediately preceding the bringing of the action and the defender consents to the granting of the decree of divorce" (s. 1(2)(d)). The Act helps to establish what is meant by non-cohabitation when it provides that, "the parties to a marriage shall be held to cohabit with one another only when they are in fact living together as man and wife"(s. 13(2)). In most cases, the couples will have separate homes. However, two people may be living under the same roof and yet not cohabiting, provided that they are not living together *as husband and wife* and such factors as the time they spend together, the nature of their relationship, financial arrangements and the absence of sexual relations, may indicate the basis of their co-existence. In one English case, the court accepted that the couple were not cohabiting when the wife allowed her sick husband to return to the family home and helped to care for him, despite the fact that she shared a bedroom with her lover (*Fuller v. Fuller* (1973)).

The non-cohabitation must be *for a continuous period of two years*, but again, reconciliation attempts are encouraged, and no account is taken of periods of resumed cohabitation not exceeding six months in all for the purpose of attempting reconciliation (s. 2(4)). Resumed cohabitation during court-ordered continuation aimed at reconciliation is not subject to any time limit (s. 2(1)). Again, no such period of time counts towards the two years' non-cohabitation (s. 2(4)).

In addition to non-cohabitation, the defender must consent to decree of divorce being granted. The defender can use consent as a bargaining tool, for example, to gain a financial advantage in the divorce. As Lord Maxwell put it, "it is perfectly open to the defender to withhold consent for any reason he thinks fit or for no reason" (*Boyle v. Boyle* (1977), at p.69). As far as the future arrangements for children are concerned, the court is bound to reach its decision having regard to their welfare, but the extent to which consent is used privately between the parties should not be underestimated.

Assuming that the parties satisfy the requirement of non-cohabitation and the defender consents to the divorce, the only defence which applies here is collusion.

Five years' non-cohabitation

Irretrievable breakdown is established if "there has been no cohabitation between the parties at any time during a continuous period of five years after the date of the marriage and immediately preceding the bringing of the action" (s. 1(2)(d)).

This ground of divorce is very similar to that providing for divorce after two years' non-cohabitation, but there are three important distinguishing features. First, and fairly obviously, the period of non-cohabitation required is five years. In computing the five years, the same periods of resumed cohabitation are permitted as were discussed in respect of two-year divorces (s. 2(1) and (4)). The second difference between the two grounds is that the defender's consent is not required in this case.

Thirdly, divorce on this ground is open to a special defence. A court is not bound to grant decree in respect of this ground "if in the opinion of the court the grant of decree would result in grave financial hardship to the defender" (s. 1(5)). Hardship is defined as including the loss of the chance of acquiring any benefit. This provision was designed to protect older spouses, and particularly older wives, who had been in long marriages where they had become financially dependent on their husbands, often because they had not pursued a career in order to raise children and run the home. In order to establish a case, the defender must establish that the grave financial hardship will result from the divorce, rather than the fact that the marriage has broken down or the parties have separated. Again, the defence of collusion could apply, but there is little likelihood of it arising. No other defences apply and, for example, the fact that the defender has a religious objection to divorce is no ground for refusing the decree (*Waugh v. Waugh* (1992)).

MEDIATION

Litigation is, essentially, adversarial and, in the context of relationship breakdown, it has long been accepted that negotiating a settlement of outstanding issues is desirable. With the emergence of mediation as an alternative, or addition, to litigation, its place in family law became obvious. While not confined to divorce, mediation offers couples the opportunity to meet with an independent third party to resolve differences and take charge of finding a workable solution. It is of particular value in helping couples, whether married or not, to make arrangements for the future care of their children, when co-operation will be crucial. However, it can also be used in respect of other matters which arise on matrimonial breakdown, like property disputes. Family Mediation Scotland and Comprehensive Accredited Lawyer Mediators (CALM), which brings together lawyers accredited by the Law Society of Scotland as family mediators, are the best known providers of mediation.

Where a dispute involves parental responsibilities and rights, a court may refer a case to an accredited mediator. Evidence of what occurred in the course of mediation conducted by an accredited family mediator is usually inadmissible in any later court proceedings (Civil Evidence (Family Mediation) (Scotland) Act 1995). Given the interest the Government has shown in mediation as a means of cutting the legal aid bill, there is a danger that we may see "mandatory mediation" (an oxymoron), at least for cases where the parties are legally aided, in the future (*Access to Justice, Beyond the Year 2000: A Consultation Paper on Civil Legal Aid* (1998)) and *Improving Scottish Family Law* (1999)).

THE PROCEDURE

Both the Court of Session and the sheriff court have jurisdiction to grant divorce, although most actions are raised in the sheriff court (Court of Session Act 1830 and Divorce Jurisdiction, Court Fees and Legal Aid (Scotland) Act 1983, s. 1). Only one of the parties to a marriage can raise an action for divorce and both parties must be alive when decree of divorce is granted. The Lord Advocate has the right to intervene in the public interest in any divorce proceedings, although this is rarely done. Where it is alleged that the defender committed adultery with a named person, the action must be intimated to that person, who has a right to intervene in order to deny the averments of adultery. Divorce cases involving children may also require intimation to relevant third parties, like the local authority if it is looking after the child. Where any order is sought in respect of the child under section 11 of the Children (Scotland) Act 1995, the action must be intimated to the child, using a special form of notice, although intimation can be dispensed with by the court. Where a request has been made for the transfer of property, under section 8(1)(aa) of the Family Law (Scotland) Act 1985, the action must be intimated to any creditor with security over the property.

At one time, the pursuer and a witness had to appear in court before a divorce could be granted. The ordinary procedure is still available and is used where the divorce itself, or some ancillary matter, like the arrangements for children or property, is in dispute. However, the vast majority of divorces proceed by way of either the affidavit procedure or the "do-it-yourself" procedure.

Ordinary procedure
The initial writ, which sets out the pursuer's case and the remedies being sought, must be served upon the defender and other interested parties. If the defender does not intend to defend the action, it will normally proceed under the affidavit procedure. If the defender intends to defend the action or any aspect of it, he or she must intimate this to the court and lodge defences, usually within 21 days (the *induciae*). If the divorce is based on two years' non-cohabitation with consent, the defender must intimate consent. The court can hear any preliminary motions to deal with such matters as sisting the action, interim residence and contact, or interim aliment. Like any civil action, an options hearing will be fixed to deal with various procedural and other matters.

Proof in divorce cases is on the balance of probabilities (s. 1(6)). Corroboration is no longer required in civil proceedings (Civil Evidence (Scotland) Act 1988, s. 1(1)), although, in establishing a ground of divorce, evidence from someone other than a party to the marriage is required (1988 Act, s. 8(3)), except when the do-it-yourself procedure is being used (1988 Act, s. 8(4) and (5)). As with other civil proceedings, hearsay evidence is permitted provided that the party who made the statement would have been a competent witness (1988 Act, s. 2(1)).

If the divorce involves a dispute in respect of children, two additional points should be noted. The first is confined to the sheriff court, and raises the possibility of an additional step in the proceedings, known as the child welfare hearing (Ordinary Cause Rules, r. 33.22A). These hearings were introduced in 1996 in the attempt to resolve disputes involving children more quickly, provided that this can be done in a manner consistent with the child's welfare. The idea here is to gather the disputing parties together and see if some or all of the disputed matters can be resolved without the need for a full proof. A child welfare hearing will be arranged automatically if there is any dispute over the future arrangements for the children and, in any case, can be ordered by the sheriff at any time, at his or her own instance. The parties, including any child who has expressed the wish to be present, must attend in person, except on showing cause why this is not possible, and all parties are obliged to provide the sheriff with sufficient information to enable him or her to conduct the hearing. The sheriff then seeks to ensure the resolution of the disputed matters and takes a more interventionist role than is usually the case in court proceedings. If the dispute is not resolved it will proceed to proof. The second point to note is that, where parental responsibilities and rights are in dispute in the divorce action, the court may refer the dispute on that point to a mediator accredited to a specified family mediation organisation at any stage (OCR, r. 33.22).

At the end of defended proceedings the court grants a decree of divorce, if the pursuer is successful, or a decree of absolvitor if the defender is successful, thus rendering the matter *res judicata*. If the action has not been defended and the pursuer has not proved his or her case, the court grants a decree of dismissal.

Affidavit procedure
Where the action is not defended, the affidavit procedure can be used and this means that there is no need for the pursuer or the witnesses to appear in court (OCR, r. 33.28). While not as cheap as the do-it-yourself procedure, it is less expensive than an ordinary proof. Unlike the do-it- yourself procedure, the affidavit procedure can be used for any of the grounds of divorce. The action begins in the same way as the ordinary procedure, with the initial writ being drafted and served upon the defender. Upon expiry of the *induciae*, the sworn affidavits of the pursuer and at least one witness are then submitted along with other relevant documents and a minute signed by the pursuer's solicitor. The court can then grant decree and the date of divorce is the date when the granting of the divorce appears in the rolls of court.

Simplified or "do-it-yourself" procedure
Where the divorce is based on five years' separation or two years' separation with consent, there is a simplified procedure which enables spouses to obtain a divorce without the need to consult a solicitor at all (Divorce Jurisdiction, Court Fees and Legal Aid (Scotland) Act 1983, s. 2.). The applicant fills out a form, available from any sheriff court, and submits it to the court along with a copy of the marriage certificate, his or her statement sworn before a notary, and the prescribed fee. Where appropriate, the other spouse indicates consent by signing the form. Unfortunately, this cheap and simple procedure is restricted to a fairly narrow range of cases since it is only available where:

(a) the application is based on one of the non-cohabitation grounds;
(b) there are no children of the marriage under 16 years of age;
(c) neither party is seeking an order for financial provision;
(d) there are no other proceedings pending which could affect the validity of the marriage; and
(e) neither party suffers from a mental disorder.

A decree of divorce granted under this procedure cannot be reclaimed against.

APPEALS AND RECLAIMING MOTIONS

Appeals from the sheriff court are heard by the Court of Session and reclaiming motions from the Outer House of the Court of Session are heard by the Inner House. Appeal to the House of Lords is possible, although rare. A decree of divorce takes effect immediately, although an extract decree of divorce will not normally be issued until the time for appeal has expired. Once an appeal has been lodged, the decree of divorce is suspended until the appeal is dealt with.

REGISTRATION

All divorces granted in Scotland on or after May 1, 1984 are registered in the Register of Divorces and an extract from the register can be obtained on payment of the prescribed fee.

Further reading
E. M. Clive, *The Law of Husband and Wife in Scotland* (4th ed., W. Green, 1997), chaps 20–23 and 27
E. E. Sutherland, *Child and Family Law* (T & T Clark, 1999), chap. 13

---

11. TERMINATION OF MARRIAGE: THE CONSEQUENCES

Marriage ends on divorce or on the death of one of the parties and there is extensive legal provision dealing with property in each case. Where the parties have cohabited outside marriage, the parties (or the survivor) must rely on the general provisions of the law as it applies to strangers. In 1992, the Scottish Law Commission recommended modest changes in the way heterosexual cohabitants are treated (*Report on Family Law*) and, again, its proposals are being discussed afresh (*Improving Scottish Family Law* (1999)). In this chapter, we are concerned solely with the termination of marriage. As we saw in chapter 9, the personal consequences of marriage are fairly limited but, when a marriage ends, these effects generally terminate. Thus, a formerly married person is free to remarry, albeit there may be some restrictions on marriage to relatives of a former spouse. What and how arrangements are made, either by the parents or by the court, for the future care of children, was discussed in chapter 5. Here our primary concern is with money and property.

FINANCIAL PROVISION ON DIVORCE

The Family Law (Scotland) Act 1985, which resulted from the Scottish Law Commission's recommendations (*Report on Aliment and Financial Provision* (1981)), provides a regime for financial provision on divorce and references in this section are to that Act, as amended, unless otherwise stated. One strength of the 1985 Act is that, for the first time, legislation sets out guiding principles, indicating what financial provision should seek to achieve, and provides the court with a broad range of orders it can make to give effect to these principles.

In an action for divorce, either spouse may apply to the court for financial provision on divorce and the general guidance given to the court is to make such orders as are *both* justified by the principles set out in the Act *and* reasonable having regard to the resources of the parties (s. 8(2)). As a general rule, the court is directed to take no account of the conduct of either party unless, "the conduct has adversely affected the financial resources which are relevant to the decision" (s. 11(7)(a)). When it is considering the fourth (facilitation of adjustment) and fifth (alleviation of hardship) principles, it must disregard conduct "unless it would be manifestly inequitable to leave the conduct out of account" (s. 11(7)(b)).

The guiding principles

The Act provides that financial provision on divorce shall be governed by the following principles.

Principle 1
The net value of the matrimonial property should be shared fairly between the parties to the marriage (s. 9(1)(a)).

During marriage, the general rule is one of separate property. On divorce, the picture changes dramatically, with *fair sharing of matrimonial property* becoming the fundamental principle. As a general rule, *fair sharing* means *sharing equally*, subject to certain exceptions (s. 10(1)). For the purpose of financial provision on divorce, *matrimonial property* means all the property belonging to the parties or either of them at the relevant date (see below) which was acquired by them otherwise than by way of gift or succession from a third party:

(a) before the marriage for use by them as a family home or as furniture or plenishings for such a home; or
(b) during the marriage but before the relevant date (s. 10(4)).

This very broad definition of property enables the courts to deal with almost everything acquired during a marriage, including what are often the largest assets the parties will have, like the home and pensions, as well as money, shares, cars and the like. It should be noted that the definition of matrimonial property here is not the same as the definition of household goods. *Students sometimes get the two confused, with disastrous results.*

Property is valued on the basis of net value at the relevant date. *Net value* is the value of the property after the deduction of certain permitted debts. The *relevant date* is whichever is the earlier of the date on which the parties ceased to cohabit; and the date of the service of the summons in the action of divorce (s. 10(3)).

Anything acquired by the parties after the relevant date, usually the date of separation, is excluded from the pot of matrimonial property, as is property acquired *by way of gift or succession from a third party*. However, such property is not wholly irrelevant, since it will count as part of the individual spouse's *resources* and, thus, become relevant when the reasonableness test is applied. So, for example, where the wife was given a flat by a third party, it was not matrimonial property, but it was part of her resources and was used to reduce the amount of capital to which she would have been entitled (*Buczynska v. Buczynski* (1989)). In addition, while such property is not matrimonial property in its original form, if it is converted into other property, it loses its protected status. Thus, for example, when donated money is used to buy property, like a house, the house becomes matrimonial property (*Latter v. Latter* (1990)). This apparent injustice is mitigated by the fact that the court has discretion to derogate from the general principle of equal sharing in certain circumstances and one such circumstance allows it to look at the source of the funds used to buy a particular asset (s. 10(6)(b)).

One difficulty arises, particularly in relation to heritage, when property increases in value after the relevant date but before the action is heard. Diminution in value will be taken into account in examining the resources available to each party (s. 8(2)(b)). Where the property belongs to only one party, he or she reaps the benefit of any gain, although that gain will form part of his or her resources. The courts had some difficulty where the property was co-owned and the solution lies in the order which should be made. In *Wallis v. Wallis* (1992 and 1993), the couple co-owned a house and it increased in value after they separated. The husband sought an order transferring his wife's share of the home to him. The Inner House and the House of Lords rejected the sheriff's solution in granting the order, and making an adjustment of capital payable to the wife to take account of the increase in value, since valuation was tied to the date of separation. Effectively, the husband reaped the benefit of the increase in value. The solution lies in refusing to transfer the property and granting an incidental order for division and sale of the property, thus enabling both spouses to share in the increase in value (*Jacques v. Jacques* (1995) and (1997)).

While matrimonial property should be shared fairly between the parties' and that usually means shared equally, the Act provides that it may be appropriate that property is shared "in such other proportions as are justified in special circumstances" (s. 10(6)) and gives the following examples of what might amount to such *special circumstances*:

(a) the terms of any agreement between the parties on the ownership or division of any of the matrimonial property);
(b) the source of funds or assets used to acquire any of the matrimonial property where those funds or assets were not derived from the income or efforts of the parties during the marriage;
(c) any destruction, dissipation or alienation of property by either party;
(d) the nature of the matrimonial property, the use made of it (including use for business purposes or as a matrimonial home) and the extent to which it is reasonable to expect it to be realised or divided or used as security;
(e) the actual or prospective liability for any expenses of valuation or transfer of property in connection with the divorce.

In making an award under this principle, the court may order the payment of a capital sum, the transfer of property, and may make an order relating to a pension (ss. 8(1) and 12(3)). It cannot make an order for the payment of a periodical allowance (s. 13(2)).

Principle 2
Fair account should be taken of any economic advantage derived by either party from contributions by the other, and of any economic disadvantage suffered by either party in the interests of the other party or of the family (s. 9(1)(b)).

Couples organise their lives in different ways and individuals make both economic and non-economic contributions, sometimes sacrificing their own economic position for the good of the other spouse or the family. This principle seeks to take account of the diversity of relationships. *Economic advantage* is "advantage gained whether before or during the marriage and includes gains in capital, in income and in earning capacity" and *economic disadvantage* has the corresponding meaning (s. 9(2)). *Contributions* mean "contributions made whether before or during the marriage; and includes indirect and non-financial contributions and, in particular, any such contributions made by looking after the family home or caring for the family" (s. 9(2)).

Advantages and disadvantages sustained, and contributions made, before the marriage can be taken into account. So, for example, where a woman gave up a job to move to be with her future husband, that could be taken into account in the subsequent divorce (*Dougan v. Dougan* (1999)). Economic advantages and disadvantages are defined as widely as possible and have enabled the courts to take account of advantage gained, for example, by having housekeeping and child care provided or receiving money or unpaid labour for one's business. The disadvantage most often recognised is the loss of career opportunities, earnings and pension entitlement when a spouse stays at home (*Louden v. Louden* (1994)).

In making an award under this principle, the court may order the payment of a capital sum and/or the transfer of property (ss. 8(1) and 12(3)), but it cannot make an order for the payment of a periodical allowance (s. 13(2)).

Principle 3
Any economic burden of caring, after divorce, for a child of the marriage under the age of 16 years should be shared fairly between the parties (s. 9(1)(c)).

Children of the marriage will need to be cared for in the future and caring for children has economic consequences. This principle seeks to share the future economic impact of child care between the parties to the marriage. For the purpose of principle 3, a *child of the marriage* includes not only children of both spouses but any child who has been "accepted by the parties as a child of the family" (s. 27(1)) and, thus, will often include step-children. In assessing the economic burden of child care, the court is directed to take a host of factors into account, including, for example, any award of aliment or child support liability and the child's age, health and educational needs. In addition, the court may take account of the fact that the payer is, in fact, supporting another person in the payer's household, whether or not there is any legal obligation to support that person (s. 11(6)). The court is directed to disregard the conduct of either party, unless it has adversely affected the financial resources relevant to the decision (s. 11(7)).

In making an award under this principle, the court may order the payment of a capital sum and/or the transfer of property and/or the payment of a periodical allowance (ss. 8(1) and 13(2)).

Principle 4
A party who has been dependent to a substantial degree on the financial support of the other party should be awarded such financial provision as is reasonable to enable him to adjust, over a period of not more than three years from the date of the decree of divorce, to the loss of that support on divorce (s. 9(1)(d)).

While much of the 1985 Act is centred on the notion of a clean break divorce, it may be unrealistic and unreasonable to expect a spouse who has been dependent on his or her partner to become self-supporting immediately. Where the division of property under the first three principles would not provide sufficiently for adjustment, this principle may be used to do so. For example, principle 4 can be used to provide a "buffer" while a spouse retrains to enable him or her to gain employment (*Wilson v. Wilson* (1998)). In assessing what, if any, order to make for financial provision under this principle, the court is, again, given a list of factors to consider, including, for example, the claimant's age, health and earning capacity and his or her retraining plans. Again, the court may take account of the fact that the payer is, in fact, supporting another person in the payer's household, whether or not there is any legal obligation to support that person (s. 11(6)). In applying principle 4, the court is given greater latitude to consider conduct. The starting point is, as before, that only conduct that affected resources is relevant (s. 11(7)). However, conduct can also be considered where it would be "manifestly inequitable to leave the conduct out of account" (s. 11(7)(b)).

In making an award under this principle, the court may order the payment of a capital sum and/or the transfer of property, although it is more usual for it to order the payment of a periodical allowance (ss. 8(1) and 13(2)).

Principle 5
A party who at the time of the divorce seems likely to suffer serious financial hardship as a result of the divorce should be awarded such financial provision as is reasonable to relieve him of hardship over a reasonable period (s. 9(1)(e)).

As we saw, principle 4 envisaged a short-term period of adjustment to independence. Principle 5 addresses the issue of past dependence, but over the longer term, and, indeed, awards here may be until the death or remarriage of the recipient (*Bell v. Bell* (1988)). It is designed to accommodate the older spouse who has been dependent through a long marriage and should be seen as a last resort. Ideally, the other four principles should be used to ensure a just result. In assessing what, if any, order to make for financial provision under this principle, the court is, again, directed to consider a list of factors, including the claimant's age, health and earning capacity and the duration of the marriage. Again, the court may take account of the fact that the payer is, in fact, supporting another person in the payer's household, whether or not there is any legal obligation to support that person (s. 11(6)). The extent to which the court can take account of either spouse's conduct, under principle 5, is the same as that under principle 4.

In making an award under this principle, the court may order the payment of a capital sum and/or the transfer of property, although it is more usual for it to order the payment of a periodical allowance (ss. 8(1) and 13(2)).

Orders the court can make
The 1995 Act expanded the range of orders the court may make with the aim of enabling it to meet all eventualities. Either party may apply for one or more of the following orders.

An order for the payment of a capital sum to him or her by the other party to the marriage (s. 8(a)).
An order for payment of a capital sum can be made on the granting of the divorce or within a period of time specified when the

divorce is granted (s. 12(1)). A degree of flexibility can be built into an order to pay a capital sum by making the order effective from a specified future date or ordering payment by instalments (s. 12(2) and (3)). So, for example, payment may be postponed until after the youngest child reaches 18 and the house has been sold and instalment payments are particularly appropriate where assets are tied up in a business which generates income. As a general rule, a capital award cannot be varied at a later date. However, where there is a material change of circumstances, either party can apply to the court to have the date or method of payment varied (s. 12(4)).

An order for the transfer of property to him or her by the other party to the marriage (s. 8(1)(aa)).

Again, an order for the transfer of property can be made on the granting of the divorce or within a period of time specified when the divorce is granted (s. 12(1)) and can be made effective from a future date (s. 12(2)). Either party can apply to the court to have the date of the transfer of property varied on demonstrating a material change of circumstances (s. 12(4)). Where a third party's consent is required before property can be transferred, as, for example, where a lender holds a standard security over the property, then the court cannot order transfer until the requisite consent has been obtained (s. 15(1)).

An order for the making of a periodical allowance to him or her by the other party (s. 8(1)(b)).

The court is directed only to make an order for the payment of a periodical allowance where orders for the payment of a capital sum or the transfer of property would be inappropriate or insufficient in the circumstances (s. 13(2)(b)). In addition, a periodical allowance may only be provided for where it is justified by principles 3, 4 or 5 (s. 13(2)(a)). Thus, the idea is that a periodical allowance should be the exception rather than the norm. An order for the payment of a periodical allowance can be made on the granting of the divorce or within a period of time specified when the divorce is granted (s. 13(1)(a) and (b)). In addition, such an order can be made after the decree is granted, where no such order has been made previously, and there has been a change of circumstances (s. 13(1)(c)). The order may be for payment for a definite or indefinite period or until the happening of a specified event (s. 13(3)). On showing a material change of circumstances, an order for payment of a periodical allowance may be varied or recalled by the court (s. 13(4)(a)) or an order for the payment of a capital sum or the transfer of property can be substituted for it (s. 13(4)(c)). Variation or recall can be backdated and the court may order money already paid to be repaid (s. 13(4)(b)). Where the payer dies, the obligation to pay a periodical allowance continues against the deceased's estate, but it is open to the deceased's executor to apply for variation or recall of the order on the basis of a change of circumstances (s. 13(7)(a)). On the death or remarriage of the payee, an order for periodical allowance ceases to have effect (s. 13(7)(b)).

An order relating to pension benefits (s. 8(1)(ba)).

A pension entitlement will often be one of the biggest assets involved in a divorce. The difficulty with pensions is that they may not be capable of being realised immediately and it may not be economically sensible to do so. The court can make an order against the trustees and managers of pension schemes requiring them to pay lump sums as directed by the court (*e.g.* to the former spouse) when they fall due (s. 12A). The following conditions must be satisfied before a court may make such an order:

(a) the court must have made an order for the payment of a capital sum by a party to the marriage (the "liable party");
(b) the liable party must have rights or interests in benefits under a pension scheme which are matrimonial property;
(c) the benefits must include the payment of a lump sum either to the liable party or on his or her death (s. 12A(1)).

Section 12A orders are subject to variation or recall at the instance of an interested party, where the liable party's liability has been discharged other than by payment by the trustees or managers of the pension scheme (s. 12A(5)). A feature of pension schemes is that rights under them can usually be transferred to another scheme, often when the member moves jobs. To take account of this possibility, regulations require the trustees or managers of the first scheme to notify the trustees or managers of the new scheme of the section 12A order and the trustees or managers of the new scheme then become liable under the order (s. 12A(6) and (8)) and the same procedure applies to subsequent transfers. The other party is also entitled to notice of any transfer of pension rights.

These arrangements, while innovative, do not provide for the more radical option of "pension-splitting". This would involve taking a part of the liable party's pension entitlement and putting it into a separate pension scheme, either with the same company or elsewhere, for the benefit of the other party. In this way, the other party would acquire a pension entitlement in his or her own right which could be enhanced by fresh contributions from that other party. Reform along these lines seems likely in the future.

An incidental order (s. 14).

In order to ensure that the courts have the broadest possible range of powers, a number of incidental orders are provided for. Incidental orders are orders for financial provision and, as such, must be justified under the principles set out in section 9 and are subject to the limitation of being reasonable in the light of the parties' resources. They include, orders for valuation or sale of property; orders in relation to the matrimonial home; and orders setting aside terms in ante-nuptial or postnuptial marriage settlements. Any of these orders, except those relating to the occupation of the matrimonial home and associated expenses, may be granted before, on or after the granting or refusal of a decree of divorce (s. 14(1)).

An anti-avoidance order.

Spouses will often be reluctant to give a soon-to-be former partner any more than they have to and some will go as far as alienating property or trying to hide assets. The court has special powers to order disclosure of resources in divorce proceedings (s. 20). In addition, the court is armed with wide discretionary powers to interdict, vary or set aside transactions aimed at defeating a claim for financial provision (s. 18). An application for variation or setting aside of a transaction or interdict must be brought within a year of the claim for financial provision being disposed of and only a transaction or transfer which took place within five years preceding the claim for financial provision may be varied or set aside (s. 18(1)). In order to be successful, it is for the challenger to establish that the transaction or transfer has had, or is likely to have, the effect of defeating, in whole or in part, any claim for financial provision (s. 18(2)). Where a third party has acquired rights in property in good faith and for value, the court is directed not to make any order prejudicing such rights (s. 18(3)). Similarly, the interest of anyone deriving title from such a third party are protected. Where the court varies or reduces a transaction or transfer, it may include in any order it makes "such terms and conditions as it thinks fit and may make any ancillary order which it considers expedient to ensure that the order is effective" (s. 18(4)).

Enforcement
Orders for financial provision can be enforced, within Scotland, using all the usual methods of debt recovery. Reciprocal enforcement within the United Kingdom is reasonably straightforward. Further afield, ease of enforcement depends on whether various international conventions apply.

Agreements on financial provision
Many couples faced with divorce will try to reach agreement on financial provision and it is highly desirable that they should avoid acrimonious and costly litigation. They may find it helpful to use the services of a mediator to assist in the process. As a matter of practice, the agreement should be as comprehensive as possible and each party should have received independent legal advice. Assuming that the couple reach agreement, they need do nothing further. However, it is common to record the terms of the agreement. Where the divorce is being pursued under the affidavit procedure or by ordinary

proof, it is usual to present the agreement in a minute, or joint minute, of agreement and ask the court to interpone its authority to it. If the parties are pursuing a divorce by the do-it-yourself procedure, the agreement should be recorded in the Books of Council and Session.

While couples are encouraged to make their own financial arrangements, the court retains the power to set aside or vary an agreement, or any term of it, where it was not fair and reasonable at the time it was entered into (s. 16(1)(b)). The court can exercise this power on granting decree of divorce, or within a time specified when the decree was granted (s. 16(2)(b)). The whole circumstances of the agreement, including non-disclosure of information and the legal advice each party received, are relevant to assessing its reasonableness. In addition, the court has the power to vary or set aside an agreement in respect of a periodical allowance: where the agreement itself provides for such variation; where the payer has been sequestrated; or where a maintenance assessment has been made under the Child Support Act 1991 (s. 16).

SUCCESSION

The law of succession merits study in its own right and only the briefest of outlines will be provided here. The Scottish Law Commission has made extensive recommendations for reform of the law of succession (*Report on Succession* (1990)) and the law may change in the future. At present, when a person dies, his or her funeral expenses and outstanding debts must be met. Thereafter, what happens to his or her property depends, to some extent, on whether the deceased dies testate or intestate; that is, whether he or she left a will.

Intestacy
In cases of intestacy, the estate is distributed as follows.

Prior rights
The surviving spouse is entitled to make three claims under this head covering: the dwellinghouse in which he or she was ordinarily resident up to the value of £130,000; furniture and plenishing therein, up to the value of £22,000; and financial provision of up to £35,000, if the deceased left descendants, or up to £58,000 if the deceased left no descendants. Where the deceased's estate exceeds the maximum value, the widow or widower is entitled to money in place of the dwellinghouse and must select which items of furniture and plenishings he or she wishes to claim (Succession (Scotland Act 1964, ss. 8 and 9).

Legal rights
After prior rights have been satisfied, legal rights may be claimed. They apply only to the remaining moveable estate and entitle the sur-

viving spouse to one-half of that, if the deceased is not survived by descendants, or one-third, if the deceased is survived by descendants. Any descendants share one-third of the moveable estate between them (1964 Act, ss. 10 and 11).

Distribution of the free estate
The remainder of the estate, known as the "free estate", goes to the first group of the deceased's relatives on the following list: children; parents and siblings (each share half between them); brothers and sisters; parents; widow or widower; grandparents; aunts and uncles (1964 Act, s. 2(1)).

Devolution of property if there is a will
Legal rights cannot be defeated regardless of what the deceased has provided for in his or her will. Thus, the surviving spouse and any children will be entitled to claim legal rights from the deceased's moveable estate. If the deceased has failed to provide for any one of them, there is no problem. However, each individual provided for in the will must choose between the legacy and legal rights (1964 Act, s. 13). A person cannot claim both. Thereafter, the deceased's property is distributed according to the will.

Neither marriage nor divorce has the effect of revoking a prior will. Where property has been left to a "husband" or "wife", or a named person, described in that way, it is a matter of construction whether a former spouse is entitled to claim (*Henderson's Judicial Factor v. Henderson* (1930); *Pirie's Trustees v. Pirie* (1962)). Unlike the courts in England and Wales, the Scottish courts have no jurisdiction to make provision for family members and other dependants where the deceased failed to do so.

Further reading
E. M. Clive, *The Law of Husband and Wife in Scotland* (4th ed., W. Green, 1997), chaps 24 and 30
E. E. Sutherland, *Child and Family Law* (T & T Clark, 1999), chap. 14

APPENDIX: SAMPLE EXAMINATION QUESTIONS AND ANSWER PLANS

Answers to examination questions should normally be written in a structured narrative unless the question indicates otherwise. In order to ensure a well-organised answer, and to make the most efficient use of limited time, an outline plan should be constructed before beginning to write the answer. Sometimes an individual will not have managed the allocated time well and will find himself or herself short of time for the last question. In this case an expanded answer plan may be accepted in substitution for the full answer, albeit the former is likely to attract a lower mark than the latter. Below, the first two questions are answered fully and the last two are answered using expanded answer plans. The answers provided assume that candidates have been given about 40 minutes for each question.

QUESTION 1

How does a court reach its decision on the residence of, and contact with, a child in a dispute between the child's parents?

Model answer (full)

In considering disputes over residence and contact, the court is directed by the Children (Scotland) Act 1995 to apply three overarching principles. Statutory references in this answer are to that Act. First, the court must regard the child's welfare as the paramount consideration (s. 11(7)(a)). Secondly, the child must be given the opportunity to express his or her views and account will be taken of these views in the light of the child's age and maturity (s. 11(7)(b)). Thirdly, the court is directed not to make any order unless to do so would be better for the child than making no order at all (s. 11(7)(a)).

In assessing what will serve the child's welfare, the court will take the individual circumstances of the particular case before it into account. This means that each case will turn on its own facts. Some idea of the facts and circumstances courts have considered to be relevant can be gleaned from past decisions. The child's basic physical welfare will be a consideration. In *Clayton v. Clayton*, the child's father made a host of allegations raising concern about the child's health and safety while in the mother's care. In the event, the court found these concerns to be unfounded and the child remained with his mother. If a parent will not be available to look after the child all the time, the court will look at the other arrangements being made, whether through day care, the provision of a nanny or the assistance of friends or relatives. In *Brixey v. Lynas*, while the sheriff's original decision was overturned on appeal on other grounds, there is an illustration of the court being influenced by the fact that the child's paternal grandmother would be playing a significant role in his life. Courts often take account of how the adults concerned will serve as role models to the child, a point illustrated by *Brixey v. Lynas* and *Casey v. Casey*. However, in the latter case, the court was at pains to point out that the relative affluence of the parties should not determine the issue.

In assessing welfare, the court will also look at the emotional dimension. In *Geddes v. Geddes*, the court took account of the fact that the child seemed to fare better in terms of school work and appetite, when in the care of his father, than he did when in the care of his mother. Just what has an impact on a child's emotional welfare is not always easy to ascertain. In *Early v. Early*, the fact that the mother was living in a lesbian relationship led the court to conclude that the child could suffer embarrassment amongst his peers, were this fact to become known. As a result, the child's father, who had convictions for child neglect, was successful in obtaining the equivalent of a residence order. Another aspect of emotional welfare is the child's relationship with other family members. As *Casey v. Casey* illustrates, the court prefers to keep siblings together and tends to favour a parent who has shown a co-operative attitude to the other parent's involvement in the child's life. The literature suggests that emotional welfare will be served by stability and, as a result, the courts are reluctant to disturb the *status quo* where it is working. This approach overlaps, to some extent, with the third of the overarching principles, which will be considered presently.

In the past, courts set considerable store by a child's spiritual welfare being taken care of and preferred a parent who would provide for this. However, the courts were consistent in their refusal to adjudicate between religions. More recently, religion has been an issue where it might have a detrimental effect on the child. For example, in *McKechnie v. McKechnie*, concern was expressed that the child might be denied particular medical treatment because of a parent's religious beliefs. The child's educational development will be considered by the court, although courts will not necessarily prefer private, over state, education (*Clayton v. Clayton*). As a general rule, the court will only be interested in a parent's lifestyle where it believes this will have an impact on the child, as is illustrated by the decision in *Early*. While in *Brixey v. Lynas* the sheriff was concerned about the mother's active social life, the Inner House attached more weight to the fact that the child was happy and settled with her. That case also raises the issue of the maternal preference. While the House of Lords endorsed its importance, subsequent courts have been able to avoid rigid application of this sexist notion (*MacMillan v. Brady*).

The second of the overarching principles requires the court to give the child the opportunity to express his or her views and requires the court to take these into account in the light of the child's age and maturity. This does not mean that the court will necessarily do what the child wants, since the child's welfare, rather than his or her views, is the paramount consideration. Taking account of the child's views often results in more weight being attached to the views of older children than those of their younger siblings (*Casey v. Casey*). In *Mason v. Mason*, the views of the elder child were sufficiently strong and clearly articulated, that she influenced the decision regarding not only her own residence, but also that of her younger brother.

The direction to the court not to make any order unless to do so would be better than not making the order places the onus of proof, on the balance of probabilities, firmly on the parent applying for the order. This point was central to the decision in *Sanderson v. McManus*, where an unmarried father was unsuccessful when he sought contact. Married parents normally have full parental responsibilities and parental rights (s. 3(1)) and the applicant will have to satisfy the court that there is a reason to restrict or remove the responsibilities or rights of the other parent. An unmarried father has no parental responsibilities or rights unless he has executed a parental responsibilities and rights agreement with the child's mother (s. 4) or has already been granted some responsibilities or rights by a court (s. 11). Thus, he enters any dispute at something of a disadvantage. However, as the House of Lords made clear in *Sanderson v. McManus*, the issue of onus of proof is usually of little practical importance when it is remembered that the court focuses on the child's welfare.

By laying down the principles to be applied, the 1995 Act gives the court clear guidance on how it should approach disputes over residence and contact. It should be noted that these principles, and particularly the first of them, is sufficiently flexible to allow the court to take the facts and circumstances of each case into account. In addition, the overarching principles, when combined with past decisions, enable legal and other advisers to assist clients in working out their own arrangements for the future care of children. Whether this is done with the assistance of mediation, or by the parties simply talking to each other, much acrimonious litigation can be avoided.

QUESTION 2

Fatima and Marcus met and married in 1965 when they were both 20-year-old medical students. They were struggling financially and Fatima gave up her studies and took secretarial work to support them. The couple had three children born in 1968, 1972 and 1975. Fatima has not worked since the birth of their first child. Marcus became a very successful consultant and now earns £200,000 per annum. When they got married, Fatima's father gave Marcus £20,000 to buy a flat. They moved to a larger house later, although the flat has been kept on and rented out. Last month, Marcus announced that he had met someone else, wanted a divorce, and moved out of the house. Fatima accepts that the marriage is over and is willing to get divorced but seeks legal advice about her financial position. Fatima doubts that she could find a job, given that her secretarial skills are very out-of-date and, in any event, she suffers from a nervous condition that would be exacerbated by working. The principal assets are:

(a) the family home worth £250,000, on which there is an outstanding loan of £50,000;
(b) the flat, which is now worth £75,000;
(c) Marcus' entitlement under his pension plan;
(d) Fatima's savings account (current balance £40,000) which is derived from money she inherited from various relatives;
(e) a Mercedes car, used exclusively by Marcus;

(f)   a VW Golf car, which Marcus gave to Fatima for her birthday two years ago;

(g)   Nermal, a two-year-old cat, which Fatima bought.

Model answer (full)

The Family Law (Scotland) Act 1985 provides a régime for financial provision on divorce and references are to that Act, as amended, unless otherwise stated. Section 9 of the Act sets out five principles to guide the court, when it is considering what orders to make for financial provision, and the Act goes on to elaborate how these principles apply and which orders may be granted in respect of each.

Either spouse may apply for various orders for financial provision and, since Fatima is seeking advice here, this answer will concentrate on what she might claim at the same time as noting possible responses Marcus may put forward. Any award must be justified by the principles set out in section 9 and reasonable having regard to the resources of the parties (s. 8(2)). Marcus may be seen as being responsible for the breakdown of the marriage. However, as a general rule, the court is directed to take no account of the conduct of either party unless it has "adversely affected the [relevant] financial resources" (s. 11(7)(a)). When the court is considering an award under the fourth (facilitation of adjustment) and fifth (alleviation of hardship) principles, it must disregard conduct "unless it would be manifestly inequitable to leave the conduct out of account" (s. 11(7)(b)). Thus, it is unlikely that Marcus' conduct will play any part in the final decision.

The first of the principles under the 1985 Act requires that the net value of the matrimonial property should be shared fairly between the parties to the marriage (s. 9(1)(a)). Before we examine how this might apply here, we must establish which property is matrimonial property. Section 10(4) defines matrimonial property as all the property belonging to the parties or either of them at the relevant date which was acquired by them, otherwise than by way of gift or succession from a third party, before the marriage for use by them as a family home or as furniture or plenishings for such a home, or during the marriage but before the relevant date. The relevant date is whichever is the earlier of either, the date on which the parties ceased to cohabit, or the date of the service of the summons in the action of divorce (s. 10(3)). Here it is the date Marcus moved out of the home. Applying the definition of matrimonial property, the house is matrimonial property. Since it is the net value of property which matters, the value of the house will be set at £200,000; that is, its market value less the outstanding loan. Whether the flat is also matrimonial property is open to debate. A similar issue arose in *Latter v. Latter* and the question is whether Fatima's father made a gift of money to Marcus, which Marcus later converted into other property (the flat), or whether the money and purchase of the flat can be viewed as a single event. In the former case the flat is matrimonial property. In the latter, since the gift was from a third party to Marcus, the flat is not matrimonial property.

Marcus' pension entitlement is relevant but only in respect of the time between the date of the marriage and the relevant date. Assuming that he only began making pension provision after he graduated, that means that the pension entitlement accrued up to the date he moved out will be matrimonial property. The £40,000 in Fatima's savings account will not be matrimonial property, since it is inherited. However, it will be taken into account in looking at the parties' respective resources. In *Buczynska v. Buczynski*, a flat the wife had received as a gift from a third party was not matrimonial property, but it was relevant in assessing her resources. Assuming that the Mercedes car was bought after the marriage, it is matrimonial property, but the court will take account of the fact that it is used mainly by Marcus (s. 10(6)). Since it is only gifts from third parties which are excluded, the VW Golf car is matrimonial property and, again, the court may take account of who uses it. Nermal the cat was acquired during the marriage and is, therefore, matrimonial property.

As a general rule, fair sharing under the Act means sharing equally (s. 10(1)). However, section 10(6) provides that special circumstances may justify deviation from equal sharing. It gives a number of examples, some of which apply here. Thus, the fact that the flat was acquired from funds provided by Fatima's father may justify her getting more than half of its value, assuming that it is regarded as being matrimonial property. The fact that the cars are used by the parties individually may justify Marcus getting the Mercedes and Fatima getting the VW Golf. The fact that the cat cannot be divided means that he will go to one or other of them, most probably Fatima.

In making an order under this principle, the court may order the payment of a capital sum, the transfer of property, and may make an order relating to a pension (ss. 8(1) and 12(3)). It cannot make an order for the payment of a periodical allowance (s. 13(2)) but, as we shall see, such an award may be made under some of the other principles.

The second of the guiding principles requires that fair account should be taken of any economic advantage derived by either party from contributions by the other, and of any economic disadvantage suffered by either party in the interests of the other party or of the family (s. 9(1)(b)). This can be used to argue that Fatima's contribution in supporting Marcus through his studies resulted in his successful and lucrative career. In addition, her role as a homemaker and child carer can be argued to have resulted in benefit to him. This view has been taken in many cases, see, for example, *Louden v. Louden*. In both cases she sacrificed her own career opportunities and lost earnings and the chance of establishing a pension. However, account should also be taken of the economic benefits that Fatima has derived during the marriage by, for example, being supported financially and having a good standard of living. It should be noted that her ill-health is not relevant here since it resulted in no benefit to Marcus. Again, the court may under this principle order the payment of a capital sum and/or the transfer of property (ss. 8(1) and 12(3)), but not a period-ical allowance (s. 13(2)).

The third of the guiding principles relates to future sharing of the economic burden of caring, after divorce, for a child of the marriage under the age of 16 (s. 9(1)(c)) and does not apply here. The fourth principle provides for short-term adjustment, for up to three years, of any award to the party who has been substantially dependent on the financial support of the other (s. 9(1)(d)). Since Fatima has little pros-pect of employment, such short-term adjustment is probably inappli-cable in this case.

The fifth principle allows for provision to be made to alleviate serious financial hardship which one party would suffer as a result of the divorce (s. 9(1)(e)). This principle is intended to provide, for example, for the older spouse in a relatively long marriage whose past financial dependence makes future independence unlikely. However, it will only arise where application of the previous principles will fail to provide adequately. In the case of Fatima and Marcus, it may be that division of the assets under the principles discussed above would mean that Fatima was facing no hardship at all. In addition, it should be noted that an award here is only justified where the serious financial hardship would result from the divorce and not some other cause. Marcus might argue that any hardship Fatima might suffer results from her health problem rather than the divorce. However, as *Haughan v. Haughan* illustrates, courts have sometimes shown sym-pathy towards older sick wives. In considering an award under this principle, the court is directed to consider a range of factors includ-ing the claimant's age, health and earning capacity and the duration of the marriage. While the court may order the payment of a capital sum and/or the transfer of property, it is more usual for it to order the payment of a periodical allowance (ss. 8(1) and 13(2)).

In summary, the court would be likely to apply the first two of the five principles and to transfer property, like the house, in order to satisfy them. It may make an award of a capital sum to Fatima and may make an order in respect of Marcus' pension. Certainly, a fairly generous award could be made in the light of the assets available and the fact that Marcus' resources are far in excess of Fatima's. It is unlikely that there would be the need to make an order for periodical allowance under the fifth principle. Of course, the couple need not go to court at all and might prefer to use mediation as a means of resolv-ing any dispute. Were they to reach agreement, this should either be presented to the court in a joint minute, in order that the court can interpone its authority, or the agreement could be registered in the Books of Council and Session.

QUESTION 3

Jenny is worried about the children, Angus, aged eight, and Flora, aged four, who live next door. The house is dirty and the garden is littered with old cars and broken machinery. During the day, the children play in the garden in all weathers and Angus is often absent from school. In the evenings, the children are sometimes left alone while their parents go out to the local pub. Jenny has tried to speak to her neighbours about matters but they have told her to "mind her own business" and she is really rather afraid of them.

Who can Jenny contact about her concerns and what might be the consequences?

Model answer (expanded answer plan)
References below are to the Children (Scotland) Act 1995.
Jenny can contact:

(a) Local authority
Wide range of duties and powers.
Duty to safeguard and promote the welfare of children in need, preferably within the child's own family (s. 22). Services for children and families. Particular relevance here—duty to provide accommodation (s. 25).
Investigate case and might seek one of a range of orders:
Child Assessment Order (s. 55): short-term measure, which can involve temporary removal of a child, to enable the local authority to assess whether its suspicion of abuse or neglect is justified—only a local authority can request a CAO and the sheriff may grant the order if satisfied: the local authority has reasonable grounds to suspect that the child is being so treated (or neglected) that he or she is suffering, or is likely to suffer, significant harm; and that such assessment is necessary to establish whether the child is being so treated or (neglected); and that such assessment is unlikely to be carried out unless the order is granted. Cannot last for more than seven days.
Exclusion Order (s. 76): exclusion of a named individual from a child's family home. Sheriff must be satisfied: that the named person's conduct threatens or is causing significant harm to the child; and that the order is (i) necessary to protect the child, and (ii) would better safeguard the child's welfare than removal of the child; and that if the order is made there will be someone who is capable of looking after the child and any other family member who lives in the household and requires care. Order must be refused if to grant it would be "unjustifiable or unreasonable". Probably not appropriate here since not clear which parent is responsible for any neglect.
Child Protection Order (s. 57): anyone can apply, but given Jenny's fear of neighbours, better to let local authority take care of it. Sheriff may grant if satisfied: (a) that there are reasonable grounds to believe that a child (i) is being so treated (or neglected) and that he or she is suffering or is likely to suffer significant harm, (ii) will suffer such harm if he or she is not removed and taken to a place of safety; and (b) that the order is necessary to protect the child from this harm. In addition, local authority may apply if its investigations are being frus-

trated. Where not practicable to apply to a sheriff for a CPO, application may be made to a justice of the peace (s. 61). Range of steps must follow—review by sheriff or children's hearing—within limited period of time if CPO granted and implemented.

Parental responsibilities order (s. 86): not a likely step at this stage.

(b) Principal Reporter/local reporters

Children's hearings system integral part of child protection. Jenny can telephone to voice concerns. Will investigate case and see whether the children may be in need of compulsory measures of supervision because one of a list of grounds may exist (s. 52). Here grounds may be lack of parental care and, in respect of Angus, failure to attend school without a reasonable excuse. If appropriate, hearing will be arranged for children. Hearing may result in supervision order.

(c) Police

Jenny can contact the police and they will look into the matter. Police officer may take children to a place of safety in an emergency, without any authority from a court, where it is not practicable to apply for a child protection order (s. 65(5)). Matter may then be referred on to reporter and/or local authority.

(d) RSSPCC and other organisations

Jenny may contact these organisations who will usually refer on to local authority and/or reporter.

QUESTION 4

Discuss the differences between nullity and divorce.

Model answer (expanded answer plan)

Nullity available in respect of void or voidable marriage. References are to Marriage (Scotland) Act 1977. Marriage may be void due to: non-age (s. 1); parties being of same sex (s. 5(4)); prior subsisting marriage of one or both (s. 5(4)); parties being within prohibited degrees of relationship (s. 2 and Sched. 1); or a fundamental defect in consent. Defects in consent are governed by the common law and include cases where a party was incapable of consenting due to insanity or intoxication or a person's consent was obtained by duress (*Mahmood v. Mahmood*). Failure to comply with formalities will not render a marriage void provided that both the parties were present at the ceremony and the marriage was registered (s. 23A). Any person with an interest may seek declarator of nullity in Court of Session and, if successful, marriage is void *ab initio*. Sole ground on which marriage is voidable is incurable and permanent impotence at the time of the marriage. Only parties may raise action and may be personally barred by, for example, adopting a child (*AB v. CB*). Voidable marriage is valid until declared void and then declarator has retrospective effect. Court can make orders for financial provision in either case.

Divorce is governed by Divorce (Scotland) Act 1976 and *sole* ground is that the marriage "has broken down irretrievably" (s. 1(1)). However, irretrievable breakdown only established by proving one of the following (s. 1(2)): (a) defender's adultery since the date of the marriage; (b) behaviour (whether or not as a result of mental abnormality and whether such behaviour has been active or passive) by defender such that pursuer can no longer reasonably be expected to cohabit with defender; (c) wilful desertion by defender without reasonable cause followed by two years' non-cohabitation during which time the pursuer has not refused a genuine and reasonable offer by the defender to adhere; (d) two years' non-cohabitation with the defender's consent; (e) five years' non-cohabitation. Different defences apply in respect of each ground and there is provision to allow for resumed cohabitation aimed at reconciliation (s. 2). Only one of the parties to a marriage can raise the action for a decree of divorce and it can be granted in either the sheriff court or the Court of Session. Decree terminates marriage from date of decree. Court can make orders for financial provision.

Differences: fundamental difference is that void marriage never existed, while divorce only available to terminate a valid marriage. Other points of difference: grounds; defences; name of decree; courts with jurisdiction; date of effect of decree. Similarities: court can determine future arrangements for children (Children (Scotland) Act 1995, s. 12) and make financial provision (Family Law (Scotland) Act 1985).

INDEX